Property of:

MW00902593

Words of Life

The Bible Day by Day
May–August 2012

**HODDER &
STOUGHTON**

First published in Great Britain in 2012 by Hodder & Stoughton
An Hachette UK company

A CIP catalogue record for this title is available from the British Library

ISBN 978 1 444 70263 7

Typeset in Sabon and Scala Sans by Avon DataSet Ltd,
Bidford on Avon, Warwickshire

Printed and bound in Great Britain
by Clays Ltd, St Ives plc

Hodder & Stoughton policy is to use papers that are natural, renewable
and recyclable products and made from wood grown in sustainable forests.
The logging and manufacturing processes are expected to conform to the
environmental regulations of the country of origin.

Hodder & Stoughton Ltd
338 Euston Road
London NW1 3BH

www.hodderfaith.com

Contents

From the writer of *Words of Life*

Faith Journey

It is wonderful to share with you, as together we fellowship in this communion with God each day in his Word. Over a period of three years we are exploring the entire Bible, seeing how God spoke to people many years ago and how he still speaks to us today. The overall theme for 2012 is 'Faith'. This edition looks specifically to our 'Faith Journey'.

We open with a series on prayer. Prayer feeds us, nourishes us. It's our daily conversation with God which strengthens us and gives wisdom for everyday life. We move from this into the book of Joshua, as the children of Israel claim the Promised Land – with God as their leader. Years later, the chosen people ask for a king. Following King Saul, David takes the throne – and they have for many years a glorious united kingdom, seen in 1 and 2 Samuel. But, because of human weakness, the kingdom begins to fall apart – as well as David's own family. Yet through it all, David draws even closer to God.

After exile, the Israelites return to Jerusalem under the leadership of Ezra to reconstruct their homeland and their lives. Then, in the book of Job, we explore one of the most profound questions of life: human suffering.

In the New Testament, Matthew unveils the life of Jesus and God's wonderful redemptive story; we also get a glimpse into the opening chapters of John's Gospel. Moving into the book of Acts, we see the spreading of the gospel and the beginning of the new Church. Our guest writer for this edition is Major Sasmoko Hertjahjo, from Indonesia, who leads us through a series relating to Pentecost.

Looking at various psalms, proverbs and hymns, we recognise how God touches our lives, wanting to work in and through us daily.

The words of life are found in God's Word, to enhance and solidify our faith journey as we walk daily with the Lord. May God richly bless you as you join the journey, meditating upon his Word in holy and divine fellowship.

Beverly Ivany
Toronto, Canada

Abbreviations

AB   *Amplified Bible* © 1965 Zondervan.

HCSB   Holman Christian Standard Bible © 1999, 2000, 2002, 2003, 2009 Holman Bible Publishers.

KJV   *King James Version* (Authorised Version).

MSG   *The Message*, Eugene H. Peterson. © 1993, 1994, 1995, 1996, 2000, 2001, 2002. Used by permission of NavPress Publishing Group.

NASB   *New American Standard Bible* © 1960, 1962, 1963, 1968, 1971, 1972, 1973, 1975, 1977, 1995 The Lockman Foundation. Used by permission.

NEB   *New English Bible* © 1961, 1970 Oxford University Press.

NKJV   *New King James Bible* © 1982 Thomas Nelson, Inc. Used by permission. All rights reserved.

NLT   *New Living Translation* © 1996, 1998 Tyndale House Publishers.

NRSV   *New Revised Standard Version Bible: Anglicised Edition* © 1989, 1995 Division of Christian Education of the National Council of the Churches of Christ in the USA. Used by permission. All rights reserved.

SASB   *The Song Book of The Salvation Army* © 1986 The General of The Salvation Army.

Prayer

'You will seek me and find me when you seek me with all your heart'
(v. 13).

Someone once said that prayer is an earthly licence for heavenly interference. In other words, we *can* make a difference when we pray. Yet what importance do we honestly place on prayer? Do we really anticipate, with excitement, our daily prayer time?

Before we can truly pray and come into the presence of God, there must be a holy fear of him, a sense of awe and wonder. And we must be a holy people. Holiness is critical for our prayer life because, as the writer to the Hebrews said: *Without holiness no-one will see the Lord* (12:14). It's the 'pure in heart' who will see God (Matthew 5:8). This does not just refer to seeing God when we get to heaven; but it has to do with our relationship, our prayer life, here on earth. We're to enter into his presence with purity of heart, living a holy life – one of integrity as a believer in Christ.

What about prayer, then? We open this devotional book focusing for a few days on the importance of prayer. I'm no expert on the subject; but I greatly value prayer and know beyond all doubt of its importance for my daily walk with Christ. I know that holiness is essential. This does not imply perfection. But I realise that having a clean heart and mind is essential if I desire to commune with my Lord.

Centuries ago Augustine prayed: 'You have made us for yourself, and our heart is restless until it rests in you.'[1] Today, I want to *rest* in the Lord, to blend my heart with his. I want to have that daily assurance that he hears my heart's cry, understands me, loves me – no matter what I do or say.

May I suggest we take a few moments, right now – whether at home, at work, or in any other place – to stop, block out all other noise, and simply *dwell* in the presence of the Almighty. Let's listen to what he wants to say to us, today.

Prayer and Repentance

Have mercy on me, O God, according to your unfailing love (v. 1).

We have done some terrible things as a human race, things that we want to erase from our memory. These things remind us of our need for corporate, as well as individual, repentance before God. In the memoirs of Elie Wiesel, Nobel laureate, he recounts perhaps one of the most evil times in human history, as a fifteen-year-old boy, arriving at the Birkenau concentration camp in Poland: 'It's a nightmare that they have torn me from those I love . . . It's in God's nightmare that human beings are hurling living Jewish children into the flames.'[2] We, ourselves, are not immune from grave sin:

For I know my transgressions, and my sin is always before me (v. 3).

Confession is a way of slicing through our defences. It's so easy to point the finger. It's innate. Our defences go up. We're not perfect, but we still think we're pretty good. However, when we truly humble ourselves, confess and repent of our sins, there is a cleansing that takes place. It goes against culture, for sin is rarely talked about. And often, when we pray, we go straight into our requests of God – neglecting to repent of our sin.

Yet, repentance brings healing. It frees us from guilt, enabling us to breathe the fresh air of forgiveness, grace, love. We need not wallow in our unworthiness, either. God's mercy comes upon us:

This is love: not that we loved God, but that he loved us and sent his Son as an atoning sacrifice for our sins (1 John 4:10).

Mysteriously, Jesus took all the hostility, evil, hatred upon himself, and redeemed it on the cross – bringing forgiveness, peace, hope.

Today, let us each pray with the psalmist:

Cleanse me with hyssop, and I will be clean; wash me, and I will be whiter than snow (Psalm 71:7).

Prayers of Thanksgiving

Be joyful always; pray continually; give thanks in all circumstances, for this is God's will for you in Christ Jesus (vv. 16–18).

It's so important to give thanks to God when we pray. To thank him for what's he's done, and for what he's going to do in the days to come. To thank him for the new day, the blue sky, the rainfall, for creation. To thank him for blessing after blessing after blessing.

We must thank God just for who he is. Praise includes this. Do we come before God with a strong sense of who he is? Can we even begin to comprehend it all? The psalmist put it this way:

Great is the LORD and most worthy of praise; his greatness no-one can fathom (Psalm 145:3).

We need to thank God for the gift of life, daily. In praising him we are to bless, worship, glorify, extol and magnify him. To be filled with a positive spirit of thanksgiving, thanking him for our health and well-being. We must not be unrealistic or false in our positive spirit – for bad things do happen to good people. Tragedies happen, sorrow may come, people get sick. But thanking him for what we *do* possess, at least for this day, is a true sign of gratitude.

We need to thank God, in our prayers, for family and friends. They're not to be taken for granted. They're to be treasured and cherished. And let's not forget to thank God for our Salvation Army corps or our church; the people of God, the community of believers. For each member helps us grow and mature in our faith.

I close with a word from Brother Lawrence. He says that prayer has to do with 'a simple attentiveness and a loving gaze upon God'.[3] May we always thank God for his loveliness, and continue to gaze upon his beautiful countenance – now, and always.

Solitude and Silence

Very early in the morning, while it was still dark, Jesus got up, left the house and went off to a solitary place, where he prayed (v. 35).

We live with a lot of noise around us. Noise on the outside; noise also inside our head. So much so that at times it interrupts our sleep, our train of thought, our equilibrium. It's difficult to find that quiet oasis amid the 'traffic' of the world that envelops us. How then do we cultivate solitude and silence in our lives?

Accomplishing this, deep within, takes both patience and practice. It's not just about the absence of sound. It's about making room, in a quiet heart, for God's presence. There's a Jewish proverb which states: 'Eloquent silence is often better than eloquent speech.' But many cultures don't do well with silence. Even in our corps and churches, silence is often very awkward. And as to solitude, we often equate this with loneliness. When alone, we wait for someone to call, drop by, invite us out. We can only take so much 'alone time'. We don't seem to think it's *normal* to be alone.

Prayer takes discipline, for these very reasons. We become distracted by the rush, by 'wordiness', by emotional clutter. How then do we silence all the raging voices within? It's interesting that, when we sit absolutely still in our heart before God, a gentle spirit of *rest* and *peace* begins to cover us. An opening of our soul.

In this kind of state, we can confront who we are in the presence of a holy and loving God. He then gently leads us in grace to a new and mysterious place. In the quietness, we can surprisingly find more energy for effective ministry.

Waiting on God isn't always easy. Yet a real sense of quietness and rest before God is essential, if we're to grow in our relationship with him. Time alone with the Almighty is essential.

Thought

Set aside some time today to be in complete silence and solitude before God. Enjoy just being in his presence in this unique way. It could be transformational.

Intercession

If we don't know how or what to pray, it doesn't matter. He does our praying in and for us, making prayer out of our wordless sighs, our aching groans (v. 26, MSG).

The word 'intercession' comes from the Latin *inter*, which means 'between', and *cedere*, which means 'to go'. To intercede then means to go between two persons in the hope of reconciling differences, or to plead with someone on another's behalf. When it comes to prayer, it means that we're to give a certain amount of time in bringing others to God in our daily conversations with him.

It's crucial to do this on behalf of friends and family. But it's also important to do this with a global perspective. Even as I write these words, I'm praying for the world at large. My mind goes from continent to continent, from country to country. Did you know you were being prayed for, specifically, sixteen months ago – at the time of this writing? And be assured, there'll be many more prayers being offered, on your behalf, in days to come. I'm just one of many praying for you. It's a glorious mystery!

It's also important to intercede for our community, right where we live. Not much can really compare with the prayer of St Francis of Assisi when it comes to wanting to be used for God's glory. Pray these words with me:

> Lord, make me an instrument of Thy peace.
> Where there is hatred, let me sow love;
> Where there is injury, pardon;
> Where there is doubt, faith; where there is despair, hope;
> Where there is darkness, light; where there is sadness, joy.

We want to be instruments, vessels, that God can use; and so we want to pray for people we know, people in our neighbourhood, people in our world. We might never know what they're going through. But God does. So we commit all people, near and far, into his loving care this day.

Prayer for Renewal

'I will put my Spirit in you and you will live' (v. 14).

We would all love to witness a revival! Yet before this can take place there needs to be renewal; for we need new strength, vision and spiritual energy infused into all of us, the people of God. This can only be done through prayer.

When we come before God in earnest prayer, asking to be a renewed people, we are seeking empowerment by the Holy Spirit. He then will answer our prayer, and we'll be renewed in a way we could never envision. As the apostle Paul said:

Inwardly we are being renewed day by day . . . So we fix our eyes not on what is seen, but on what is unseen (2 Corinthians 4:16, 18).

Perhaps we can't identify in words the change taking place within us. We might not be able to tell another person exactly what has happened to us that's made us different. For when we ask for renewal, we're asking to be transformed within:

Be transformed by the renewing of your mind (Romans 12:2).

Why do we want this? So that, through our renewal, through our mysterious and mystical transformation, we can be more like Jesus. When this happens we, and all those who pray in a similar way, are ready for revival. We're ready for the 'bones' of Ezekiel's vision to come alive, and be on fire for God. We *will*, indeed, live!

Are we ready for this? For a revival within ourselves and consequently in our corps and church? Pray that these things will happen, and that they'll become a reality. It can all begin right now . . . in prayer.

Prayer

'Yours, O Lord, is the greatness and the power and the glory and the majesty and the splendour, for everything in heaven and earth is yours' (1 Chronicles 29:11). Today, and in the days to come, may my prayer life be rich, O Lord; for in sharing my heart with you, I will grow to be more like your Son, Jesus Christ.

Meditation

Do not let this Book of the Law depart from your mouth; meditate on it day and night, so that you may be careful to do everything written in it (v. 8).

As we begin looking into the book of Joshua, it's interesting to note that it's the first in a group called the 'Former Prophets'. Along with Judges, 1 and 2 Samuel and Kings, they trace the history of Israel from the entrance into Canaan in the thirteenth century BC until the exile from the same land in the sixth century BC. This history, written for religious reasons, shows how God deals with his people. Here one sees the tremendous respect for the law. Obedience to it was paramount, for it virtually meant obedience to God himself.

God had promised his people an inheritance, a land they could call their own. They were now on the brink of claiming that land of promise, Canaan. But first they needed to be strong and courageous; they needed to be obedient by meditating on God's Word – day and night.

Joshua was their new leader, succeeding Moses. He'd been chosen, commissioned and assured of God's presence. Coming out of slavery in Egypt, he'd been an eyewitness to all God had done through his predecessor. He was a skilled person – leading in victory against the Amalekites; and he was a man of great faith as he voted with the minority to invade Canaan. Yet he still needed to meditate on God's Word. For ultimately, this was the only means for success, for victory.

There can be negative connotations with the word 'meditation'. But the *right* kind of meditation is powerful, essential; it's life-giving. For it is meditation upon God's holy Word – absorbing it, drinking it in, praying it through, living it out; it's trying to understand what God was saying *then*, and what he's saying *now*.

Prayer

Lord, I *do* want to feed and *meditate* upon your Word day and night. Fill my mind and heart with your holy presence.

The Scarlet Cord

So she sent them away and they departed. And she tied the scarlet cord in the window (v. 21).

The Israelites were preparing to move into the new land. But they had to make sure they did it in the right way, to execute the invasion properly. Spies were sent ahead to investigate. Joshua knew that Jericho had to be captured, to gain access to the various road passages. These spies were to see how this could be done effectively. And so they followed a woman, Rahab – a harlot of Jericho – to her house, located on the city wall.

The people, even the king himself, knew where the spies had gone. He demanded that she expose them. But she denied knowing of their whereabouts, fully convinced that it would be futile to fight against the God of Israel. Even if the spies were caught, Jericho was doomed because of God's ultimate plan for his people.

So Rahab quickly allowed them to escape, having faith that one day she and her family would be spared. Hope – for a 'woman of the night', a foreigner, an alien. Her faith was that strong. She put the scarlet cord in her window.

Hope. Redemption. Eternal life. Sometimes we might feel there isn't much hope for certain individuals who have made poor choices in life. Yet Christ says that salvation is available to *all* people. We are to reach out, telling as many as possible of this great hope, this possibility of new life in Christ.

The Salvation Army's Founder, William Booth, put it this way:

> God wants to live with you, not only in your home, but in your very heart. Poor and ignorant as you may be among men, and little noticed, nay, even despised, by the great and rich people of the world, yet God – the great God, whom the 'heaven of heavens cannot contain' – wants to come and live in your heart, and that not as a visitor only, but as an abiding guest.[4]

May the scarlet cord be a symbol of our faith and hope in Christ's redemptive work in our lives this day.

Amazing Things!

Joshua told the people, 'Consecrate yourselves, for tomorrow the LORD will do amazing things among you' (v. 5).

Today's verse implies two things: preparation and anticipation. Two important words; yet do we always prepare well, then anticipate with excitement? How well, really, do we prepare ourselves for what's to come today, or tomorrow? And how often do we actually anticipate God's promises?

Preparation. Joshua told the Israelites they needed to consecrate themselves. They needed to fully prepare themselves spiritually for what was to come. What did consecration involve then, and what does it involve now? When God asks us to prepare ourselves, to consecrate ourselves, what does he expect from us?

I believe he wants us to praise him, glorify his name, spend a few moments just thanking him for who he is. He then wants us to confess any wrongs (both sins of commission and omission); to ask for forgiveness with humbleness of heart. We're to bring petitions before him, trusting him with our concerns; therefore, leaving anxieties and worries with him. Then we're to ask him if there's anything he wants us to do for him, making ourselves available for service. Finally, we're to invite afresh the Holy Spirit to come upon us, to wash over us with his holy presence.

It really doesn't take long to prepare ourselves. And then what?

Anticipation. What amazing things could happen to us today? God will cause the sun to rise – another brand new day. He will show to us the flowers in the field that delight and bless us. He'll let us hear the children laugh and play, bringing a smile to our face. God will call to mind our family, who mean so much to us. God will 'speak' to us, through his precious Word. And at the end of the day we'll see the twinkling stars, which bring such a sense of peace.

Let's be sure to consecrate ourselves this day. For, no question, some amazing things are in store for us!

Genealogy

A record of the genealogy of Jesus Christ the son of David, the son of Abraham (v. 1).

The book of Matthew is an exciting Gospel, for it's filled with God's story – just for us! As the first book of the New Testament, it opens up new thought, new inspiration, a new way of looking at God and what he's done for each one of us.

At the commencement of the book we're a bit dumbfounded by the genealogy. Often it's tempting to skip these opening verses. We don't find a genealogy in the other Gospels, so conclude it's not important. Basically, a tabulation of names from the past.

The word 'genealogy' can also mean 'genesis'. The book of Genesis traces the creation of the universe and humankind. Matthew is now showing that the advent of Jesus is the inauguration of a 'new creation'. Right from Abraham's call, God has been moving to accomplish his wonderful redemptive plan for all people.

This genealogy also speaks of obedience, listing names of those who responded to God's direction in their life: Abraham, Ruth, David, Hezekiah, Josiah, Joseph. And yes, even names such as Tamar and Rahab! God works in mysterious ways when speaking to, and through, his people – from all kinds of backgrounds.

I recall a woman who was new to our Salvation Army corps (church). She radiated God's love and never hesitated to tell others of Christ. Her last name was Booth. I asked her if she'd looked at her genealogy, to see if she was related to our Founder, William Booth. 'Oh, yes,' she said, 'I am well aware of my background. I'm related to the Booth who assassinated Abraham Lincoln!'

We may have a great genealogy behind us – spiritual people who have nurtured us and helped us become the people we are today. But there may be some dark or shady characters there also! God has somehow used them all to bring us to where we are today. He's created us for such a time as this.

We're to be obedient to whatever he asks of us, for we're part of *his* genealogy. We're part of the lineage of the King of kings!

Dreams

After Herod died, an angel of the Lord appeared in a dream to Joseph . . .
'Take the child and his mother and go to the land of Israel' (2:19, 20).

Mary, a beautiful young virgin who loved God with all her heart, was found to be 'with child'. This happened through the miraculous visitation of the Holy Spirit. Joseph was no doubt totally confused, probably in denial – so decided to quietly break the engagement, the betrothal. But, an angel came to him in a dream, confirming all that Mary had told him:

What is conceived in her is from the Holy Spirit (1:20).

The Magi came to Bethlehem, but were warned in a dream not to go back to inform Herod; for instead of him wanting to visit the baby, he wanted to kill the child. The Magi took another route home. Then an angel came again to Joseph – in a dream – telling him to quickly escape, for Herod was determined to find them. They left in the middle of the night for Egypt, staying there until they heard of Herod's death. In yet another dream Joseph was told by an angel to pack up and return to Israel; to go north to Galilee. They settled in a town called Nazareth.

While studying at a seminary recently, I took a course which addressed the subject of dreams. The professor told us to write down our dreams for two weeks, then determine how God may be speaking to us in our dreams. An interesting exercise! And in many ways very revealing and eye-opening. Personally, I know that God *did* speak to me in a profound way through this simple exercise – in a way I'll never forget.

Dreams can indeed be powerful. It takes great discernment to know what they mean, what they're saying to us. May we *always* be ready to hear God, then be obedient to his direction and gracious prompting.

Thought

For at least one week, try writing down your dreams – even if you have to jot them down in the middle of the night! Then ask God if he has something he wants to say to you, specifically relating to your dreams.

Help, Lord!

The words and promises of the Lord are pure words, like silver refined in an earthen furnace, purified seven times over (v. 6, AB).

The Hebrew hymnal, the book of Psalms, contains many laments – this being one of them. David looked out at a world that seemed to be in opposition to everything he believed in. People not caring for the oppressed, the poor; in fact, people consumed with cynicism and hatred, mistreating and abusing others less fortunate. His human response was to seek God's vengeance upon them:

Help, Lord! For principled and godly people are here no more; faithfulness and the faithful vanish from among the sons of men (v. 1, AB).

He saw the deterioration of his generation. The more he tried to tell them of God and of his faithfulness, the more people seemed to live according to their own laws and practices. It was making a mockery of the very God David loved with all his heart.

There's a story told in Greek mythology of Sisyphus, the legendary founder of Corinth. He once greatly offended Zeus and, as punishment for his offence, had to push a huge boulder up a mountain. Once at the pinnacle he had to let it go, and then start up again from the bottom – for eternity. Futility; extreme frustration; endless despair. This is how King David felt, in trying to reach out to his people, witnessing the abuse and mistreatment of those more powerful upon their subjects – the poor, the fragile of society. It was ungodly.

However, God responded to David's cry with the word *justice*. He would protect those abused, and keep them safe. And his promise was pure, true – giving David renewed hope and faith in his God.

Prayer

Today, I invite you to pray for people who are abused – that they will find renewed hope, renewed faith. We must also pray for the ones mistreating others – that they will come to see the light of Christ.

I am Praying

At that moment heaven was opened, and he saw the Spirit of God descending like a dove and lighting on him (v. 16).

> I am praying, blessèd Saviour, To be more and more like thee;
> I am praying that thy Spirit Like a dove may rest on me.
>
> (*SASB* 584)

It's a wonderful privilege to pray, isn't it? To commune with God, daily. And it's so important to pray with a humble and contrite heart. As Fanny Crosby has penned in this beautiful hymn, we pray to be *more and more* like Jesus; that his Spirit would *rest* upon our very countenance. Why do we need this assurance of God's presence within us? Because all of us have needs, troubles, anxieties, worries – and God knows about them all:

> Thou who knowest all my weakness,
> Thou who knowest all my care,
> While I plead each precious promise,
> Hear, O hear, and answer prayer! (refrain)

Today in Canada, and in many other countries around the world, it is Mother's Day. Today, I want to honour my mother, a retired officer, almost ninety years old. I could mention many of her wonderful qualities – selfless, giving, caring, loving; a true role-model for my life. I'm humbled to be her daughter. But above all, she is a woman of prayer. She lost her husband, my dad, nearly twenty years ago – just when she had her leg amputated because of cancer, causing other physical ailments.

But her prayer life has never wavered. Although she often says she 'can't do much' any more, I remind her that *prayer* is the most precious gift she can give us, and all those she prays for on a regular basis.

I love her, with all of my heart, for who she is – God's child, my mom. I want my prayer to be like hers, reflected in this last verse:

> I am praying, blessèd Saviour, And my constant prayer shall be
> For a perfect consecration That shall make me more like thee.

Dry Sandals

The priests who carried the ark of the covenant of the LORD stood firm on dry ground in the middle of the Jordan, while all Israel passed by until the whole nation had completed the crossing on dry ground (v. 17).

As we continue in the book of Joshua, we note that God specialises in dry sandals. He loves to start with impossible situations in life – then do the *impossible*. The nation of Israel approached the Jordan, after fully consecrating themselves. They were ready; so God told them to move forward. The priests were in the front; more than a million people behind. Would they step forward into the flood-swollen river? A miracle would happen, *only* if they took the first step.

I'm sure they took a very deep breath, then moved. The waters immediately rolled back. The puddles even dried up. The people were kicking dust as they crossed. For the ground was not wet at all. In fact, their sandals were completely dry as they walked.

Faith requires that great initial step. It's huge. Think about what we are facing, even today. Maybe it's something to do with health – for ourselves, or someone close to us. Maybe it has to do with someone's salvation – a child's, a friend's. Maybe it's something to do with work or a friendship. Perhaps it's something very deep that we can't share with anyone else. It's so private.

Whatever it is, God wants us to face it and to move forward. Not alone, but with him. He wants us to experience that 'dry sandals' experience, which can only happen if we take that initial leap of faith. It takes great courage and trust.

God wants to delight us, to surprise us! Things might just turn out in a way we never expected at all. Yes, the sandals will still be dry – for God goes ahead and prepares the way.

Thought

God will not lead us to any waters he cannot part. Let's reach out today and speak to someone who is facing a Jordan River experience. As we do this, let's remind that person of who else walks with them.

Memorial

'Tell them to take up twelve stones from the middle of the Jordan from right where the priests stood and to carry them over with you and put them down at the place where you stay tonight' (v. 3).

Yesterday has meaning for today. It's important to recall things from the past, to help us with what's happening in the present. We're to look back with a sense of deep gratitude for what God has done, in order to do well today. We look back to appreciate all we have. It's not dwelling in the past, but rather keeping alive experiences that have happened, to ensure a better today and tomorrow. It's a memorial; a remembering.

The Israelites were instructed to take a stone – not from the riverbank, but right from the middle of the Jordan where the priests had stood. Not just one stone, representing the whole group; but twelve stones, representing each tribe, each section, each grouping. For they accomplished the crossing of the Jordan as a nation. Everyone participated. It was to be a corporate memorial, an act of worship, together. It was to be a testimony to God's presence with them, his intervention, his miracle.

It's interesting, reading the account of the crossing. Let's imagine the waters held back on either side, in order that we can cross. Would there be a sense of panic? Apprehension? Fear? Yet none of this is recorded. The people just marched forward, fully trusting that the waters surrounding them would hold until all were safely across.

The ark of the covenant was seen by all. God's presence. When everyone had crossed, the very first thing they did was to erect an altar. Thank you, God, for our deliverance!

Many monuments are erected, past and present, to honour people's achievements. More monuments need to be erected, to honour all that God has done for us.

Thought

Today, perhaps you can go to a place where there is somewhere to pray; or right where you are can be an altar, an erected monument, a place of prayer that has meaning for you. God will honour your devotion to him!

Face Down

Now when Joshua was near Jericho, he looked up and saw a man standing in front of him with a drawn sword in his hand . . . The commander of the LORD's army replied, 'Take off your sandals, for the place where you are standing is holy' (vv. 13, 15).

Joshua and the Israelites were now ready to conquer Jericho. Yet the battle would obviously take much courage, strength, strategy, and combined effort on the part of the people. They knew it had to happen – if they were to claim the land. As Joshua was preparing his mind, heart and spirit for all of this, he suddenly encountered a man with a drawn sword. At first he didn't know who he was, so asked:

'Are you for us or for our enemies?' (v. 13).

The man identified himself as the commander of the Lord's army. Some call this encounter a theophany, or a Christophany. No matter the term, it was definitely an appearance of the Lord. He was ready to fight the battle *with* Joshua – alleviating all fear.

Fear can grip us, even paralyse us. Fear of small things that creep into our lives; fear of the big things: a new kind of work, the future, sickness, death. Yes, we all have faith. Yet why then the fear?

Joshua didn't ask for a sign, to our knowledge; but God knew he needed one. As the 'man' identifies himself, Joshua's response is to fall *face down* (v. 14) in total reverence. He was then told to take off his sandals, for the ground where he stood was holy – similar to God's encounter with Joshua's predecessor, Moses, at the burning bush.

Face down. Perhaps not in public but in private, when it's just us and the Lord, it's worth trying. It's a humbling experience. Shoes off; in complete humility, in total worship. It's an experience not to be forgotten. For once we know he's with us, and he knows we are totally depending upon him, then we are ready – for whatever lies before us.

'This is My Son'

'This is my Son, whom I love; with him I am well pleased' (v. 17).

Continuing with the book of Matthew, we soon realise we know very little about Jesus' childhood. Apocryphal writings fill in certain details, to be believed or not believed. Scripture only tells us of when he was twelve, at the temple.

When God knew the timing was right for Jesus' public ministry, he used John the Baptist to prepare the way; a man who was bold, unique in style and dress. He called out for renewal. John seemed to have introduced the idea of baptism by water, to symbolise repentance and cleansing. And he talked much about the coming Messiah, the King – who would inaugurate a new kingdom. He quoted from the prophet Isaiah:

'Prepare the way for the Lord' (v. 3; Isaiah 40:3).

John also told his followers that the coming Messiah would baptise with the Spirit – far superior to his baptism with water. This 'fire' baptism meant that one would be under a superior influence:

'He will baptise you with the Holy Spirit' (v. 11).

'With' the Holy Spirit, it says. It's not 'of' the Spirit; not something the Holy Spirit does. Rather, it's the gift of the Spirit himself. Yes, there are things the Holy Spirit *does* for us: regeneration *of* the Spirit, illumination *of* the Spirit, the anointing *of* the Spirit. But being baptised *with* the Holy Spirit is God coming upon us, his gift to us – something John the Baptist couldn't give.

As John was speaking, Jesus came to be baptised. Then, the Spirit of God came upon him, like a dove, 'lighting' on him. God spoke of his great love for his Son. When we are baptised *with* the Spirit, God then says to us, 'You are my son, my daughter, whom I love.'

What is our response to his love for us, today?

Sermon on the Mount

Now when he saw the crowds, he went up on a mountainside and sat down. His disciples came to him, and he began to teach them (vv. 1, 2).

J esus was presenting his 'platform'. It was his statement of life. It was his statement of heaven, his summary of his preaching. It was his message for all to hear; for then, for now. It was foundational, this Sermon on the Mount. How I wish I'd been there – to hear it all from him! To hear him deliver the Beatitudes:

Blessed are the poor in spirit . . .
Blessed are those who mourn . . .
Blessed are the meek . . .
Blessed are those who hunger and thirst for righteousness . . .
Blessed are the merciful . . .
Blessed are the pure in heart . . .
Blessed are the peacemakers . . .
Blessed are those who are persecuted because of righteousness . . .
Blessed are you when people insult you, persecute you and falsely say all kinds of evil against you because of me (vv. 3–11).

We, who might humbly identify with one or two of the above, are truly *blessed* by God. This is deep stuff. Some say the Church is superficial. There is nothing superficial about the Beatitudes. They are at the very heart of Christ's teaching. They beckon us to be committed followers of him. The key point is to realise Christ died to enable us to live out this Sermon on the Mount, which includes these Beatitudes, in day-to-day life.

The world desperately needs *true* Christians; people who desire to follow God's lead. For when we are indeed being obedient to him, we are blessed – and so are others, as they see Christ's light shining in and through us.

The Beatitudes are at the beginning of Christ's teaching, for they are fundamental. If we don't get this part right, we won't get anything else right. And our reward? The kingdom of heaven; comfort; inheriting the earth; being filled; mercy; seeing God; called his sons and daughters; heaven. Can we ask for anything more?

Survival

*How long, O L*ORD*? Will you forget me for ever? How long will you hide your face from me? (v. 1).*

The lines from the opening of Psalm 13 reflect real desperation. Grief, pain, loneliness. For it was written by King David when his son, Absalom, not only turned on him but actually drove him from his throne and kingdom. This was an extremely dark time for David, as you can imagine. His heart was broken. He felt totally defeated, abandoned, to the point of even his faith being shaken.

David seemed to be on the threshold of depression here. Those who struggle with this terrible affliction – and many do – know the symptoms. Some describe it as if a black curtain is covering their whole being. The weight of it all, almost unbearable. The bleakness, the suffocation.

David was definitely going through these deep feelings. Many of us can't imagine what it would be like for our child to turn on us to this extreme. Yet in saying this, many of us can identify with certain darkness and despair at least to some degree. When it happens we desperately seek a way out.

It's hard to admit we're sinking, making ourselves vulnerable. And it's hard to imagine any sense of reversal to our situation. But David did the right thing. He *did* reach out, crying to God for help. For, deep down, he knew God wouldn't abandon him:

But I trust in your unfailing love; my heart rejoices in your salvation (v. 5).

Failure and defeat are so difficult; the feeling of total abandonment, so devastating. Pain hurts. Tragedy surrounds us. We wonder sometimes how we'll ever survive. Yet we also know that God *is* with us. Let us claim David's final affirmation for ourselves today, and share it with someone else who is going through a difficult time. There *is* survival – for those who trust completely in him:

*I will sing to the L*ORD*, for he has been good to me (v. 6).*

We are Blessed Indeed!

Blessed are those who dwell in your house; they are ever praising you (v. 4).

There is a beautiful Salvation Army song, or hymn, based on the Beatitudes, that simply reminds us of how blessed we are as believers in Christ:

> Blessèd are the poor in spirit, They the Kingdom shall possess;
> Blessèd are the broken-hearted, They shall not be comfortless;
> Blessèd are the meek and lowly, Theirs the earth by right shall be;
> Blessèd they who thirst for goodness, They shall drink abundantly.
> (Arch R. Wiggins, *SASB* 95)

We live in a world that equates happiness with wealth, fame and power. But Jesus came to earth to speak of a far deeper joy; to acknowledge *all* people, no matter their race, status or economic situation. All are to be blessed. It comes down to the matter of the heart. We are promised that those who are right with God will one day see him. The opening lines of verse 2 of the song say:

> Blessèd are the men of mercy, They shall fear no threatening rod;
> Blessèd are the pure in motive, They shall see the face of God.

Imagine – seeing the face of God! And yet, are we always pure in our motive? Do we always do things, never expecting or desiring praise, thanks or acknowledgement? It's something to really think about. From time to time we've all fallen short, I'm sure.

In the last verse, the song speaks of those who suffer for Christ's sake:

> Great is your reward in heaven, For the prophets' marks you bear;
> They who suffer persecution Shall the prophets' blessings share.

Many of our brothers and sisters have experienced terrible persecution, all for believing in Christ. One day they'll receive their reward, as promised by Jesus. When you stop to think about it all, we have to admit we *are* a blessed people indeed!

That's the Spirit!

A Pentecost series by guest writer Major Sasmoko Hertjahjo

At the time of writing, Major Sasmoko Hertjahjo is Literary and Editorial Secretary for The Salvation Army's Indonesia Territory and also serves as the territory's Director for Legal and Parliamentary Matters and Child Protection Issues. After receiving a Bachelor of Engineering degree in 1984, he was commissioned a Salvation Army officer in 1987 and, with his wife, served in various corps (churches). Other appointments have been as a school supervisor; at the Army's officer training college; as projects officer at territorial headquarters; in youth ministry and then as a divisional secretary. The major gained his Bachelor of Theology degree in 2006.

Introduction

In the popular Salvation Army musical *Spirit* one of the songs asks a number of questions – then gives the same answer to each one:

> Who is it tells me what to do and helps me to obey?
> Who is it plans the route for me and will not let me stray?
> Who is it tells me when to speak and what I ought to say? . . .
>
> Who is it shows me what to be and leads me to that goal?
> Who is it claims the heart of me and wants to take control?
> Who is it calls to holiness of body, mind and soul? . . .
> That's the Spirit! Holy Spirit!
> That's the Spirit of the Lord in me!

> (John Gowans, *SASB* 204)

In this series of readings for the weeks before and after Whit Sunday, guest writer Major Hertjahjo addresses some of these questions in relation to the person and purpose of the Holy Spirit. The major uses passages from John's Gospel, Acts and Galatians to help our understanding of important facets of the Holy Spirit's ministry in and through believers' lives.

Life and Rebirth

'You should not be surprised at my saying, "You must be born again"'
(v. 7).

Sin came into the world. Because of this, people often cannot feel or think rationally. They do not claim faith in Jesus Christ. Humans tend to do evil, which leads to suffering. Perfection and glory from the Lord is nowhere to be seen. The light has gone out. Because of certain misdeeds, the potential in people has vanished. Their lives seem futile.

Crimes, such as human trafficking, are results of people living without Christ. People without him don't behave in the right way. They show how a life is lived separately from God. Is God really going to let this go on and on? No, God has initiated repair and restoration. This is the premise of the New Testament: life and rebirth.

The apostle Paul emphasised that God, according to his time, has fulfilled his promises through his Son, Jesus Christ, to restore human life (see Galatians 4:4, 5). So when Nicodemus spoke about Jesus' power and strength, Jesus answered that a renewed life is the answer to people's problems. We must be 'born again'.

A renewed life is a 'must' when a person is willing to reunite with God and be restored. Life will be better than before. It begins with our returning to God, followed by the continuing work of the Holy Spirit. Then our life will be sanctified and flawless before God. A renewed life can create a renewed environment and, moreover, a renewed world. Changes like this will only happen if we are renewed by the Lord. To be born of both water and spirit means to be cleansed by the Holy Spirit and to be pure within.

Do we want to make things better? Let us each begin with ourselves.

Prayer

Dear Lord, my God, pardon my sins and my wrongdoing. I surrender to you totally. Cleanse me with your Spirit, so that I will be renewed.

Worship and Renewal

'God is spirit, and his worshippers must worship in spirit and in truth'
(v. 24).

In her conversation with Jesus, the Samaritan woman explained the
Samaritan way of worshipping God on the mountain, as instructed by
Moses years before:

When the LORD your God has brought you into the land you are entering to
possess, you are to proclaim on Mount Gerizim the blessings (Deuteronomy
11:29).

All they wanted to do was be obedient; to express their love and thanksgiving
to God, and to give him honour and praise for who he was. Jesus responded
by saying that worship is not about sacrifices given in certain places, but
rather worshipping in spirit and in truth.

We are reminded of some other Old Testament verses:

'The multitude of your sacrifices – what are they to me?' says the LORD.
'They have become a burden to me; I am weary of bearing them'
(Isaiah 1:11, 14).

Jesus told the woman that worship must come from the heart.

The Samaritan woman knew of the coming of the Messiah; once he came,
he would explain everything to her and her people. The hour had come; and
the time was now. Jesus simply said:

'I who speak to you am he' (John 4:26).

The renewal for worship began in the presence of Jesus. When we worship
him with all our heart and are led by the Spirit, this is true worship. It is to be
reflected in our daily life – in all we say and do.

Prayer

All my heart I give to you, Lord, day by day. Help me always to worship you in
spirit and in truth.

Holy Spirit – Source of Life

'The Spirit gives life; the flesh counts for nothing. The words I have spoken to you are spirit and they are life' (v. 63).

Life is essential; without it, we have nothing. Yet many people waste their lives, failing to bring forth fruit. They put constant blame upon others for their circumstances. Because of various attitudes, often their lives become miserable and depressing.

Life is about the physical world; but it is also about the spiritual world. We must bring a certain balance to our lives in all we do, so that one aspect does not take over the other. It is important to have shelter, food, work; but there is so much more to life than this.

Jesus was surprised at the response of the people, and their incapacity to understand the meaning of *eternal* life. They enjoyed eating the loaves and fishes he provided for them; but there was more to life than eating. Food is not the source of real life. The Spirit gives life; the Spirit is, in fact, the *source* of all life.

The goodness of life lies entirely with God. The Holy Spirit, when we accept Christ as our Saviour, permeates our being – making our life whole. This is what true life is all about. Because of our faith in Christ, we will live eternally. There may be hardships and trials, but we will be able to cope if we obey him and rely on his Spirit.

That we have such a wonderful God is hard to comprehend! He simply asks us to meditate upon him, and to trust him with the difficult and challenging times.

When we live by faith in him, the Spirit of God will give us strength, day by day, to cope with all that happens. The Holy Spirit is the source of life. Despite our fragile flesh and fleshly desires, if we put our trust in Christ his Spirit becomes the fountain of life and strength for us. He is our Source, our Life!

Prayer

O God, Holy Spirit, I give you my life. Abide in me always, and help me to know daily your strengthening support.

Holy Spirit – Water of Life

'Whoever believes in me, as the Scripture has said, streams of living water will flow from within him' (v. 38).

It is somewhat difficult for some people to understand similarities between spirit and water. Spirit is invisible, as is breath. However, if you blow on something, the presence of breath is evident. Breath gives life. Water, on the other hand, is a liquid. It is a clear substance that you can see, feel and taste. It also gives life, for every creature, every plant, needs it. Two thirds of the human body consists of water. When this amount decreases, the body weakens – which can eventually lead to death. Just as we need water, and air to breathe, so too do we need the Spirit of God in order to live.

When speaking to the crowd during the celebration of the Feast of Tabernacles, Jesus uses the analogy of water to explain the function of the Holy Spirit, to share how vital this is for life itself. The Holy Spirit makes life meaningful and full of purpose. Jesus invites those who are really 'thirsty' to come to him, to drink. When people believe in him, he says, their hearts will swell like rivers of living water, empowered by the Holy Spirit.

There is life abundant for those who accept Christ, all because of the Holy Spirit coming upon them. This abundance includes love, wisdom, a caring spirit, a sense of justice, peace, and the strength to carry one another's burdens. There comes a certain tranquillity within; for Christ's life, his words, are filled with truth. It is for us, and for others. We can be God's instruments to reach out and bless others. We can lead them to Jesus, who will – by his Holy Spirit – transform their lives.

This living water, the Holy Spirit, flows for all who are obedient to him. How beautiful are the lives of those who are blessed, and who continue to bless others. The Holy Spirit *is* the Water of Life!

Prayer

Lord Jesus, I believe in you and surrender my life to you. Fill me with your Spirit, that I may be a blessing to you and to others.

Baptised with the Holy Spirit

'For John baptised with water, but in a few days you will be baptised with the Holy Spirit' (v. 5).

One of the most important doctrines of the Bible is the baptism of the Holy Spirit. This baptism is crucial in the life of the believer, in order to cultivate faith and build a better relationship with God. Baptism of the Spirit is key to church growth. History records that people filled with the Spirit are successful in their ministry.

Baptism of the Holy Spirit is different from water baptism. Water baptism, for the Church at large, is a sign of repentance and confession to Christ as Lord and Saviour. Baptism of the Holy Spirit, on the other hand, is not just a sign or a confession of Christ; it is the fulfilment of all God wants and has for us. Once we are baptised with the Holy Spirit, our hearts are set on serving and worshipping God alone. We have a desire within to give ourselves fully to the testimony of Christ for the sake of others – that they might also find salvation.

At a banquet, the night before Jesus ascended into heaven, he asked his disciples to remain in Jerusalem. They were to wait for the Father's promise of the baptism of the Spirit. This baptism of the Holy Spirit would be God's seal of approval upon them, as they were getting ready to do great works and ministry for him.

Through this baptism the Lord equips believers with the gifts of the Holy Spirit, giving them courage to testify about Christ – his work of salvation, for all humankind. God also desires that his people are zealous for his great works, while remaining humble, and glorifying his name at all times.

We need to guard this baptism well. We need to pray, read Scripture and meditate upon the Lord, living holy lives as we develop our relationship with God. We must never take it for granted.

Prayer

Lord, lead me and guide me, so that I may live a life of righteousness and holiness. May your Holy Spirit baptism be evident in my life always.

The Power of the Holy Spirit

'But you will receive power when the Holy Spirit comes on you; and you will be my witnesses in Jerusalem, and in all Judea and Samaria, and to the ends of the earth' (v. 8).

The key objective of the baptism of the Holy Spirit is to give the disciples and believers authority to testify boldly about Christ and his work of salvation. The Holy Spirit would enable them to help those who were lost and gone astray, to show them the way of salvation. The Holy Spirit would speak through God's people, telling them of the possibility for new life in Christ. The ultimate goal was for Christ to be known, adored, praised and glorified.

We read in Acts the stories of believers and their courage in testifying about Christ. Jesus affirms that the Holy Spirit will give to all who believe in him this same authority – 'in Jerusalem . . . all Judea and Samaria', but also to the whole world. His power encourages believers to testify boldly without fear. We are not to be afraid, for Jesus promised:

'The Holy Spirit will teach you at that time what you should say' (Luke 12:12).

Authorisation demonstrates power at work and produces an influential dynamic. The power of the Holy Spirit is strong and infinite. Jesus announced to his disciples that, once they received this power, nothing would stop them from witnessing and testifying. The authority given by the Holy Spirit drives out demons and evil spirits; it also heals the sick, and brings encouragement to others. Our words and deeds are a testimony, when coupled with Christ's love and justice. All is for the glory of God.

We need to give all to Christ. When we do this, the power of the Holy Spirit will come, freeing us to do all God wants us to do for him. He wants our humility, and he wants our full surrender.

Prayer

Lord, I realise I am nothing without you. I am powerless to testify without the power of your Holy Spirit. Fill me, Lord Jesus.

Revolution Begins

Suddenly a sound like the blowing of a violent wind came from heaven and filled the whole house where they were sitting. They saw what seemed to be tongues of fire that separated and came to rest on each of them (vv. 2, 3).

Pentecost, the feast of thanksgiving or harvest, was a celebration for all Jewish people. They were to bring their first harvest to God. But this particular Pentecost festival would turn out to be a historic day for the Church and all Christian believers. This is the day the Lord poured out the 'fire' of his Holy Spirit upon all the believers who were gathered in Jerusalem. Fire, symbolising purification, was separated upon each one. This same fire *burned* into them, so that they could speak new tongues and speak great things about God's plan for all people.

The fulfilment of the Holy Spirit on that day is the fulfilment of prophecy – equipping the disciples with power from on high. It has become an important moment for all of us, because now every believer is able to express their faith and proclaim Jesus Christ as the source of life and salvation. That day, the number of people who were saved was great, because of what happened. Their lives were changed from worldly people to spiritual people. The same is possible for today.

The revolution begins. It started with those who were present on that day. Throughout history courageous people have preached the gospel. People have died for their faith, because they wanted only to obey Christ. They were zealous in their faith, and wanted only to live for Christ. And the revolution is to continue.

The Holy Spirit burns, generating transformation. When we are filled with the holy fire of God, we want to bring transformation to others. Are the 'signs and wonders' evident in our lives today?

Prayer

I thank you, Lord, for the gift of salvation. Give me the Spirit of Pentecost, so that I will be encouraged to preach your Word and bring salvation to all.

His Time Has Come

'In the last days, God says, I will pour out my spirit on all people. Your sons and daughters will prophesy, your young men will see visions, your old men will dream dreams. Even on my servants, both men and women, I will pour out my Spirit in those days, and they will prophesy' (vv. 17, 18).

The pouring out of the Holy Spirit to believers in Jerusalem at Pentecost was all part of God's plan. This was the right time for God to bestow salvation upon all people through Jesus Christ. It was not limited to the Jewish people. The prophet Joel had prophesied about what would happen. Peter stood and firmly defended that the believers, who had been accused of intoxication, were speaking in foreign tongues about Christ, according to the gift of language given to them by the Holy Spirit.

The New Testament reveals that the last days will start with the coming of Christ, with the outpouring of the Holy Spirit upon believers – sons, daughters, men, women, servants – and they will end when Christ returns for the second time. It will be the ushering in of the new kingdom of Christ, condemning all evil. The coming of the Holy Spirit did not stop at Pentecost. It will continue, until Jesus Christ comes again.

Today is the day for the Lord to pour out his mercies to all people; for now is the time to be saved, and to be filled with the Spirit. The power and the blessings of the Holy Spirit are being poured out in abundance to all, before the return of Christ. The Holy Spirit works through his people, his servants, to bring about salvation for all. This is how the Church of Christ is to grow. When God is at work, nothing can stop him.

The outpouring of the Spirit is upon all believers, including us, today. But have we used this to preach Christ to others and for God's glory? Only you can answer this. His time has come for us to act according to the will of the Holy Spirit.

Prayer

Lord, I do not know how to speak, nor do I have enough courage to preach the gospel of your salvation. Fill me with your Spirit, and give me courage to testify to the lost.

Dare to Speak the Truth

'For we cannot help speaking about what we have seen and heard' (v. 20).

No one is able to put a stop to the truth of the Lord, when it is being revealed by the Holy Spirit. When God's people are trusting in God, and speaking the truth in his name, nothing can stop this. Whether people hearing the message choose to believe it or not is another matter. But the truth of God can never be covered up.

Here, in this passage, Peter and John were before the Sanhedrin. The authorities were desperately trying to stop their preaching. But the two disciples responded with these words:

'Judge for yourselves whether it is right in God's sight to obey you rather than God' (v. 19).

It took courage to tell out the truth. But they could do it, for they were filled with the Holy Spirit. They lived the truth, and would not compromise it, nor cover it up. They dared to risk their lives for it. This was and is a great paradigm shift for all believers. Even when opposition came, they refused to give in:

'Salvation is found in no-one else, for there is no other name under heaven given to men by which we must be saved' (v. 12).

Throughout the ages the Holy Spirit has encouraged and inspired believers to testify about the truth of the gospel of Christ to all people. Those saved are because of the Spirit's work in their lives. It is because of people who dare to speak the truth.

Today, with the world getting more and more secular, many people do not believe in God. They do not understand salvation; yet God still calls out to them, wanting to fill them with his Holy Spirit. Do we dare to speak the truth of God with others?

Prayer

Holy Spirit, enable me to speak for God, testifying to his truth – until the end of time.

Holy Spirit – the Key to Success

This proposal pleased the whole group. They chose Stephen, a man full of faith and of the Holy Spirit; also Philip, Procorus, Nicanor, Timon, Parmenas, and Nicolas from Antioch, a convert to Judaism (v. 5).

When the number of those being saved increased greatly, it was wonderful news; but the workload of the ministry became too heavy. The apostles were zealous in their preaching of the gospel. Progress in the ministry was taking place. Yet many were being neglected, such as the widows. This caused discontent. The apostles needed to take action; and so they wisely chose others – deacons – to carry out the administration. This enabled them to carry on preaching and teaching. People were still being saved.

There were special requirements for these newly appointed deacons. The main emphasis was that they were filled with the Holy Spirit, and were both wise and faithful. These stipulations were important in light of those who needed extra love and care. They needed to have patience, and be both faithful and honest in all they did. The deacons had to have a good reputation, ready to pray for people at any time. This delegation of work was essential for the apostles; for the work of evangelism and social service was and is important for increasing the numbers of those being saved.

The key to success in ministry is that the Holy Spirit be free to work through the lives of believers. He needs to be allowed to take control of people's lives, in order that God's work be done. When we are humble before God, allowing God's Holy Spirit to work in our lives, there will be staggering results. We need to be obedient to whatever God asks of us, so the Holy Spirit can work through us. For when this happens, people will be saved, and the Church will grow. The Holy Spirit is the key to success in our ministry.

Prayer

Lord, you know me. Forgive my vanity, and teach me always to be humble. Give to me your Holy Spirit, so I can work harder for the salvation of others.

Filled with the Spirit – Destroying the Flesh

For in Christ Jesus neither circumcision nor uncircumcision has any value. The only thing that counts is faith expressing itself through love (v. 6).

The apostle Paul explicitly explained to the Christian community in Galatia that Jesus Christ had freed them from sin and punishment. This gift was theirs, because they had faith in Jesus. They no longer lived by the law given by Moses, but by the law of Christ. They no longer lived by the will of the flesh, but by the will and leadership of the Holy Spirit. Their lives were now fully controlled by the Holy Spirit, who promised to direct them, and help them live in the truth.

The nature of the flesh includes all thoughts, desires and evil deeds – anything that wanders from God's Word. This includes sexual immorality, impurity, lust, idolatry, sorcery, enmity, strife, jealousy, anger, selfishness, betrayal, factions, envy, drunkenness, debauchery, and so forth. Those who lead such lives will not inherit the kingdom of God. God is not pleased with such a way of life, for it destroys his perfect creation of humankind.

The Holy Spirit, who dwells in the heart of a Christian, will drive out such evil thoughts, desires and deeds from a person. Their life will be completely under the power of the Truth, and evil thoughts will vanish from the heart.

The problem lies in the fact that we live in a damaged world. Can we really resist all forms of evil happening around us? Isn't it impossible to live right before God? The answer is that it *is* possible to live a holy life, all because of the power of the Holy Spirit. He works in us, to make us righteous – giving to us the capacity to resist the sins of the flesh, and to drive out all evil. Those who believe in Christ have the Holy Spirit to resist evil.

Prayer

Almighty God, fill my life with your Spirit, so I may faithfully abide in your will and resist all sin.

True Christians are Fruitful!

But the fruit of the Spirit is love, joy, peace, patience, kindness, goodness, faithfulness, gentleness and self-control. Against such things there is no law (vv. 22, 23).

The Holy Spirit, who fills the lives of believers, not only has the power to drive out sinful thoughts and deeds; he is also powerful in actually destroying the power of sin itself, which is the source of all bad behaviour. Instead, the Holy Spirit desires to completely overhaul the lifestyle of believers, so they live honest, sincere and holy lives.

When this happens, and their lives are no longer hypocritical in any way, they begin to produce the fruit of the Spirit. It becomes the way they think and act, all in harmony with God's holy Word. They no longer compromise with sin and its devious ways. This past lifestyle has been crucified. Their lives depict righteousness, and there is no longer anything false.

The fruit of the Spirit is demonstrated through genuine love and caring for others, with no strings attached. A believer's life becomes filled with joy and peace, despite still facing challenges and temptations. The believer is filled with patience and is able to maintain self-control when slandered, reviled or accused of committing wrongful acts. They remain strong when faced with difficulties. The believer obeys only the leadership of the Holy Spirit, therefore making their life respected before God and others.

Such a life is ongoing, for the Holy Spirit encourages them to continuously practise or demonstrate the characteristics of the Holy Spirit in their life. Nothing can now hold them back. The Spirit-filled life is a life that brings about the fruit of love, truth, justice and peace. This is true Christianity.

Prayer

Father God, I open my heart and my life to you. Fill me with your Spirit, always. For without you I would not be able to produce the fruit of the Spirit, the fruit of righteousness, in my life.

Holy Spirit – the Helper

'I will ask the Father, and he will give you another Counsellor to be with you for ever – the Spirit of truth. The world cannot accept him, because it neither sees him nor knows him. But you know him, for he lives with you and will be in you' (vv. 16, 17).

Jesus called the Holy Spirit 'Counsellor', the 'Spirit of truth'. These names denote both his nature and activity. He is one who comforts, and also one who assists and helps. He is an advocate, intercessor, friend. According to his name, everything he does is all about truth. He encourages believers to live according to all truth, and to bear much fruit.

Jesus understood his disciples, knowing them far better than they knew themselves. He knew it would be difficult for them when he was no longer with them. As the great Teacher and the Good Shepherd, he did not wish for them to believe in false teachings, or to go astray. He did not want them to fall short of their life goals in him, or not to find happiness in Christ. So Jesus prayed to his Father that another Comforter would come to be with them, guide them, and help them conform to God's will. He assured the disciples that the Holy Spirit would abide with them and dwell within them. This truth was for them – and it is for us today as well.

Jesus lived, helping and strengthening his disciples. He comforted, counselled and defended them in times of trouble and affliction. He became their friend, saving all those who believed in him. The Holy Spirit comes to each of us, comforting, counselling. He is our friend. He reveals to us the truth of God, helping us at all times.

This same Holy Spirit encourages us to be obedient to God. He sees corruption in the world; he sees temptation all around; he sees disobedience and sin. He wants to be our helper in such a world, and desires to rest in our heart – revealing to us only God's truth. We can count on him, if we obey God's holy will for our lives.

Prayer

Holy Spirit, forgive me for all my sins. Dwell in me, and help me to live according to God's perfect will.

Holy Spirit – Holy Life

'But the Counsellor, the Holy Spirit, whom the Father will send in my name, will teach you all things and will remind you of everything I have said to you' (v. 26).

Jesus explained to his disciples that the task of the Holy Spirit was to teach them all things, and to remind them of his teachings. Later in John's Gospel he also said:

'When he comes, he will convict the world of guilt in regard to sin and righteousness and judgment' (16:8).

This verse is also very important. Believers are to commit fully to the Lord, living a life of holiness and righteousness. Many still live in sin. Many deny Christ, going their own way. They do not believe that Christ came to save humankind and reconcile them to God. People today think they are fine to live life as they want to live it. They refuse to believe in God's way, and in God's holiness.

God protects his people. He has, from generation to generation. It is not the will of God that anyone be lost. It is not his will that we be caught up in sin, and the pollution of the world. Through his Holy Spirit he desires to illumine the minds of his people so that they will understand his Word. He wants to lead them into all truth. The Holy Spirit wants everyone to live holy lives; to turn from the temptations of the world, and desire only him. He wants us to only glorify Christ.

God's truth leads us to this holy life. If we are obedient to his teachings, rejecting sinful thoughts and actions that produce sin, the Holy Spirit will free us. He wants to dwell in each of our hearts, so we can promote Christ's holy way of life. He wants to dwell in our hearts, so we can live a life of holiness for our God.

Prayer

Dear Lord, and precious Holy Spirit, I am unworthy. I cannot live a holy life without you. God, remain with me and guide me always.

Walls

When the trumpets sounded, the people shouted, and at the sound of the
trumpet, when the people gave a loud shout, the wall collapsed (v. 20).

Returning to the book of Joshua, we see that the Israelites were given *specific* instructions: when they marched around Jericho seven priests, with seven trumpets from rams' horns, were to be followed by the ark of the covenant. In front and behind were to be armed guards. And so the Israelites left camp, marching around the city walls for six days, blowing the trumpets. It's what God said; and so they obeyed.

On the seventh day they were to march around the city seven times. Then on that seventh time, following a loud blast from the trumpets, the people were to shout loudly – for they knew then that the city would be theirs, given by the Lord. They did what was asked of them. When they shouted, the walls of the city collapsed.

These were *divine* instructions. Even though the instructions might have seemed rather odd, the people were obedient and victory was theirs. Everything was destroyed; all but Rahab and her family, identified by a scarlet cord. Spared, because of her faith in God.

God gave to his people *life-giving* instructions. The presence of the ark was fundamental; for it showed, through it all, that God was with them. He told them that if they followed his lead, they would conquer what lay before them; they'd have life, a future.

Walls. Have you ever felt there were walls in front of you, blocking you from moving forward? Have you ever 'hit a wall', preventing you – or so you thought – from progressing? This is when we need God more than ever. This is when we need to bring whatever is hindering us and lay it before Christ, asking for specific, divine, life-giving instructions. What does he want me to do? How am I to deal with this situation, enabling me to move forward in my faith?

God wants us to break down any walls, trusting him completely. Sometimes the walls may be daunting, even frightening, as they appear before us. This is when we need to trust him. For with him, the walls *will* collapse, they *will* go away – but only by his grace. Let us hold on to this truth and live it out accordingly; then, share this good news with someone who needs to hear it today.

Secrets

But the Israelites acted unfaithfully in regard to the devoted things;
Achan . . . took some of them (v. 1).

God's only warning to the Israelites, in taking the city of Jericho, was to
not take any of the 'devoted' or sacred things for themselves. All the
silver, gold, bronze and iron articles were to be saved in the Lord's treasury.
But Achan, from the tribe of Judah, had a secret. He saw, and he took. No
one would ever know – or so he thought. It had been far too tempting for
him; and after all, he only took *some* for himself. Just a bit. A secret sin.

Yet one man's sin affected the whole group. It's interesting to note the
Bible recording, as we've read today, that the Israelites as a people were seen
to have acted unfaithfully – even though it was actually only one man who
had that secret and sinned. Yes, everyone suffered because of it. Several verses
later we read that many Israelites in fact died, all because of that one sin.
Suffering, pain, defeat, repercussions – for the whole.

God went as far as saying Israel had 'violated' his covenant (v. 11). Again,
all because of one dirty secret. Then God further states:

'I will not be with you any more unless you destroy whatever among you is
devoted to destruction' (v. 12).

Pretty frightening words! Pretty serious business! But then he gives a solution:
to consecrate themselves fully to him, afresh. To get rid of any secrets and
come clean before him, in all humility. How? Clan by clan, family by family,
person by person.

Secrets, although fun in some instances, are not to be held if they hurt or
harm others, or damage our relationship with God in any way. We cannot
come before a holy God holding on to any sins we know have not been
acknowledged, confessed and forgiven.

At the commencement of this new day, let us make sure we are not
harbouring any secrets that are, in fact, sins. Rather, let's confess, seek
forgiveness, and start the day as a new and cleansed person in Christ – having
the assurance that God *is* with us!

The Altar

Then Joshua built on Mount Ebal an altar to the LORD (v. 30).

The altar is a sacred place. It's a place where we can come to give thanksgiving to God. It's a place where we can seek forgiveness, can claim the blessing of holiness. It's a place where we can renew our covenant with the Lord. Yes, an altar is often used in our church for these very purposes. But an altar can be 'built' anywhere. There doesn't even have to be a physical structure of any kind. It can be in our home, or in an open space. It's where we come before God in worship.

In the Scripture passage for today, Joshua erected an altar on Mount Ebal. Years before, Moses had instructed the people never to forget the importance of worshipping and giving thanks to God. Joshua felt this was the time and place to do just that. Four things took place: he built the altar, a meeting place for God and people; offerings were brought – things, yes, but also a fresh offering of themselves; instruction was given, for hearing from God was essential; then finally they practised certain rituals, not for the sake of the rituals themselves but rather to help newcomers like Rahab feel welcomed and accepted.

All these things took place around the altar, for it was a holy place; a place where God met with his people. It was where the people renewed their covenant with God, where they communed with God in an intimate way.

Many of us attend church and are fully aware of the altar there. No doubt we have used it personally on many occasions. If we haven't in recent days, perhaps it might be a place we would want to visit soon. But also, it's important to have an 'altar' in our home. A family altar; a personal altar. These altars can be set around a meal table; or it can be a chair, a bedside. It might even be a moveable altar. The important thing is to *have* a place where we worship God; a place where we speak, heart to heart, with the Almighty. Once established, as a sacred 'ritual', that time alone with the Master will be like no other. So, let's pray . . .

Three Words: Just Do It!

'You are the salt of the earth . . . You are the light of the world'
(vv. 13, 14).

Have you ever made reference to someone being 'the salt of the earth'? If so, you probably meant they were solid in character, genuine in personality, goodness personified. When we think of salt itself, we think of preservation and flavour. In the Roman world, it also symbolised purity – from the process of using sea water and the sun to acquire salt. Roman soldiers were often paid in salt, the basis for the word 'salary'. Therefore, when Jesus used the symbol of salt, he no doubt thought of Christians living pure and holy lives. They were to infiltrate society, preserving this pure life in all things. They were to keep the flavour of joy in their Christian lives.

Jesus also said we were to be lights in a dark world. Light symbolises radiance, joy, illumination. We are to be witnesses for Christ, always. Not bringing attention to ourselves; but rather, pointing the way to God and his goodness.

In recent times, in the Church at large, there has been much emphasis on 'being' rather than 'doing'. Of course, we are to *be* people of God, people of character, people of integrity. But we can *also* be people who are not afraid of getting into the world and sharing life with others. Three words to living a wholesome life, as witnesses for Christ, are: 'Just do it!'

So often we procrastinate. So often we think others will do it; or that we can do it later, when the time is right. But God wants us to be in his world, seeing what needs to be done – and then to just do it! To be the salt and light he spoke about more than 2,000 years ago. Not seeing them as goals to be achieved, or seeing people as projects; but simply being Christ to others in need. Just do it. Are you up for the challenge?

Thought

Think of something, someone, needing special attention. Think of the three words, 'Just do it!'; then be the salt and light God wants you to be, for him, today.

Revolutionary Thinking

'But I say to you, do not resist an evil person; but whoever slaps you on your right cheek, turn the other to him also' (v. 39, NASB).

Have you ever been treated unfairly? Or have you ever been bullied, or abused, or been the object of cruel behaviour? If so, how have you felt inside – and how have you reacted? Human nature tells us to give it back. An eye for an eye, a tooth for a tooth. It actually goes back to not only the Old Testament, but also the Code of Hammurabi, dated circa 1780 BC. Vengeance and revenge have been part of people's lives from the very beginning. And this oldest law in the world – called the *Lex Talionis*, parochially referred to as tit for tat – was what made the revenge legitimate.

But Jesus appeared, with revolutionary thinking! He said to resist retaliation. In fact he said, when slapped on the cheek, to give the person your other cheek. Was this masochistic? No, not at all. In fact, quite the opposite. He was giving us the freedom to live by his direction. To be free from having our behaviour determined by the way we are treated. To live by the higher law of love. To respond in a manner reflecting complete freedom in Christ, embracing his limitless love.

This passage, then, is the essence of the Christian ethic. It is how we, as Christians, are to react to others. To live in peace with all people. To overcome evil with good. Jesus' thinking was indeed revolutionary, for it was contrary to all the base instincts lying within us. It's about loving those who hate us; forgiving those who harm us; blessing those who are against us. It's about love, emerging from within – all because of God's grace. It's about freedom, and mercy, and salvation.

Jesus came to change our way of thinking, completely; our way of living out life. Revolutionary indeed! And so, the next time someone does something to us that's not good, let's really think about how we will respond. May it be with God's grace and love. May others see Christ in us.

Generation to Generation

Above all else, guard your heart, for it is the wellspring of life (v. 23).

The first part of Proverbs 4 is very personal, as are many other opening chapters from this book of wise counsel. For they are from father to son; from parent to child. Gentle, yet firm in instruction. It's about how to get the most out of life; to live the right way, according to God's plan and desire for us.

In this particular proverb, the father speaks to when he was a boy himself, and how his father commanded him to attain wisdom and understanding. It speaks to the value of seeking godly wisdom:

Love her, and she will watch over you (v. 6).

The second part of the chapter speaks to giving advice, parent to child. It stresses the importance of living a good and righteous life; accepting instruction from the right people, and learning from it. When one lives a life that is wise and good, it reflects God's light:

The path of righteousness is like the first gleam of dawn, shining ever brighter till the full light of day (v. 18).

The final part of the chapter speaks of guarding one's heart, for there are so many things in the world which not only distract us, but actually steer us off the course God has planned out for us. We are to keep our eyes fixed on him, and on his desire for our life:

Let your eyes look straight ahead, fix your gaze directly before you (v. 25).

Wisdom passed on – from generation to generation. How vital this is! To receive; then, to pass it on to generations following us. May God continue to keep us open to hearing from him, and from others, always.

Take My Life

'Consecrate yourselves and be holy, because I am the LORD your God'
(v. 7).

Frances Ridley Havergal, living in the nineteenth century, began writing poetry at the age of seven. She had an insatiable thirst for the Bible, memorising the entire New Testament, along with the Psalms, Isaiah, and the Minor Prophets. Unbelievable! She was also a contralto soloist and a brilliant pianist. At the age of fifteen she gave her life to Christ.

When aged twenty-one, Frances was at an art gallery in Germany, staring at a picture of the crucifixion. Underneath the painting were engraved the words: 'This I have done for thee; what hast thou done for me?' Tears streamed down her face. From that moment on, she gave all her talents to the service of Christ.

> Take my life, and let it be Consecrated, Lord, to thee;
> Take my moments and my days, Let them flow in ceaseless praise.
>
> Take my hands, and let them move At the impulse of thy love;
> Take my feet, and let them be Swift and beautiful for thee.
>
> *(SASB 525, vv. 1, 2)*

Frances was frail physically, yet managed to write beautiful songs. Today's hymn was her prayer of thanksgiving and commitment. Despite her suffering, and eventual death at the early age of forty-two, she lived out her prayer, for she was fully devoted to her Lord:

> Take my will, and make it thine, It shall be no longer mine;
> Take my heart, it is thine own, It shall be thy royal throne. (v. 5)

May her prayer be echoed in our hearts this day. Whatever we have, may it *all* be given over in complete devotion to our Lord.

> Take my love; my Lord, I pour At thy feet its treasure-store;
> Take myself, and I will be Ever, only, all for thee. (v. 6)

Inheritance

Now these are the areas the Israelites received as an inheritance in the land of Canaan (v. 1).

East of the Jordan, Moses had given land to the Reubenites, the Gadites, and the half tribe of Manasseh before his death. Then, the Israelites went into the promised land of Canaan to conquer Jordan. It was now time to divide the land, west of the Jordan, for the remaining tribes. It was to be according to the inheritance God, their Father, had provided for them.

This new land was just for them, and they were now ready to receive their promised inheritance. It was an exciting time, as they waited to hear the news. A time of great anticipation. What would the possibilities ahead look like? What could they *do* with this new land? How would this God-given inheritance play out in the future for them?

It's wonderful to receive an inheritance – usually from a parent, or a close relative. Of course, with it come many memories of the 'giver'. But it's wonderful to realise that this same person has desired to *bless* you, by giving something tangible; not only as a remembrance of them, and the affirmation that you played a significant role and part in their life, but also something to be of benefit to you in the days that lie ahead.

Many times, the Israelites were reminded of their history. But now, they were in the land he'd promised them. God had been faithful in the past; and he would be faithful in the future as well. In this new land, each tribe was given a parcel of land they could call their own. It was their inheritance; it was to be a treasured gift from God. It was the first of many wonderful things God would do for them in this land they could now call home.

And for us today, God gives us a wonderful inheritance:

The promised Holy Spirit, who is a deposit guaranteeing our inheritance until the redemption of those who are God's possession (Ephesians 1:13, 14).

May we embrace this day, using it only for his glory and honour!

Promises

Not one of all the LORD's good promises to the house of Israel failed;
every one was fulfilled (v. 45).

We have all made promises. Hopefully, most of them we have kept. However, some might have been broken, or not fulfilled, due to unforeseen circumstances. People also make promises to us. We hold on to these promises dearly. But sadly, sometimes people break them – with no explanation given, no sign of regret. This hurts deeply. And for many, it's hard to move forward.

Here in this passage of Scripture we are told that God has been faithful to his people. He made certain promises to them and we're told *all* were fulfilled. None failed. And the wonderful news is, God is the same today as he was then. When he promises to be with us, through *all* things, we can count on him without question.

This assurance builds our faith. His faithfulness is foundational for our belief in him. His timing might be different from ours; but he always answers our prayers. It might be a different answer from what we think best; but we must trust him with the outcome. For he knows all things – beginning to end.

When we read today's reading it's interesting to note that not all of the land in Canaan had been conquered. Yes, the various tribes were given their allotment; but there was still much work to be done, land that still needed to be taken. It's the same with us today. Yes, we believe in Christ, often thinking that because of this belief all will go smoothly. Yet there will no doubt still be battles to be won, 'land' to be conquered. But the beautiful promises of God keep us moving forward – with the comfort of knowing his everlasting presence with us.

As we come across the various challenges that may face us today, let's hold firmly to this promise, as recorded in Scripture:

The LORD gave them rest on every side (v. 44).

May you find rest in him today – knowing his promises are sure.

Soul Thoughts

After a long time had passed . . . Joshua, by then old and well advanced in years, summoned all Israel (vv. 1, 2).

I invite you to pause for a moment, right now. Take a deep breath. Now, another one. Inhale slowly; then, even more slowly, let the breath out. No one's looking, so don't feel self-conscious. I'm doing it too, as I write. Enjoy the awesome gift of breath itself, of life. Indulge me again. Take another deep breath, then let it out.

Too busy to waste time doing this? I know the feeling. Perhaps we're *all* too busy. Too often we operate at a frantic pace, caught up in a whirlwind of constant, pressured activity. We desperately try to meet the expectations of others upon us, and in so doing virtually fragment ourselves in the process.

Could things be different? In the Middle East there's an estimated 15,000 Bedouin shepherds, each living to an average of more than 100 years old. Why such longevity? What's their secret? It appears to come down to the lack of stress in their lives. By all accounts, they seem very happy and contented. They know no other lifestyle.

Joshua summoned his people together. He really had nothing *new* to say to them. He was only anxious, as a very old man, to speak to them from the heart; to pass on some deep 'soul thoughts' – in order that the children of Israel stay true to God. They had all fought hard and long in battle. And there was still more to do. But it was important to take time to reflect, to take that deep breath, to appreciate and value life itself, to stop and give thanks to God for his abiding presence. Enfolded into these same soul thoughts was the challenge to never take God for granted; for once we take our eyes away from him, we will fail and be completely lost.

Joshua's charge to his people can be taken as a charge to us all. As we take that deep breath, as we strive to slow down – taking stock of what we're doing and *why* we're doing the things we do – let's hear Joshua's words and embrace them in all we say and do today:

Be very careful to love the LORD your God (v. 11).

Judging Others

'Do not judge, or you too will be judged' (v. 1).

There is a distinct difference between discernment and judgment. Discernment is an important and necessary gift to be used within the body of Christ. Christian love should not be blind; and discipline is often necessary. But judgment is something quite different. It's so easy to point the finger. Do we ever do this? It's so easy to criticise another person. Yet what is our personal motivation behind the criticism?

We are meant to serve and help others; to see them grow in grace as we grow ourselves. When somebody messes up, we are often quick to judge. And when it's another Christian, are we even more prone to judge and put them down? Sometimes we think by doing so, we make ourselves look better. But often it's quite the opposite.

Only God sees another's motivation. Maybe there are things going on that we know nothing about. Maybe they are reacting out of something being done to them. Often we say we need to speak the truth 'in love' to someone. But is it always done *in love*? It's critical to do a check on ourselves. It's also vital to allow God to see what's within – in order that a valid self-examination takes place.

It comes down to the attitude of our own heart. We can't expect mercy from God if we're not ready and willing to be merciful toward another. We are so prone to being blind to our own failings, then intolerant of the vices of others. Maybe it's actually that we see something of ourselves in the wrongdoing of another. Perhaps this is really why we are so quick to judge, even condemn.

May we be more open to others, to their shortcomings. May God have mercy upon us, for all we have done to break his heart.

Prayer

Lord, so often I am quick to judge. Help me to be more tolerant of others; to be wise, but not to jump to conclusions so quickly. Help me to love my fellow brothers and sisters better, as you love them – and as you love me.

The Cost of Discipleship

'Follow me, and let the dead bury their own dead' (v. 22).

Matthew records ten miracles in chapters 8 and 9, demonstrating Jesus' power over disease, the forces of nature, and the spirit world. Jesus then bestows the same power and authority on his chosen apostles – sending them out as ambassadors of the kingdom. In doing this, he also warns them of the possible dangers they will face, calling them to committed discipleship.

The essential characteristic of the Christian life *is* discipleship. We are to live under Christ's Lordship, daily following his direction. Yet with this comes a cost, a price to pay. Dietrich Bonhoeffer, a great theologian of the twentieth century who *did* pay that price at a very young age, said: 'Only he who obeys truly believes, and only he who believes truly obeys.'[5] Obedience is a response to God's grace, no matter what the cost; for disciples, regarding Christ as their model for all ethical directives, *want* to obey him.

When reading today's Scripture, you might think Jesus was not being very empathetic. One of the disciples wanted to follow Jesus, but first asked to bury his father. Certainly we can identify with the man and his situation. Yet in the context here, the disciple was really asking to stay and fulfil the occupational expectation of his father before getting up and following Jesus – which might have meant delaying for many years. Christ's mission was for right then; it is for the now! The response Jesus gives is a word-picture. In other words, let that which is part of the old life die; it will take care of itself. Instead, Jesus wants us to follow him – and live!

It's about priorities. Are we willing to follow Jesus, no matter the cost? Ready to give up certain personal dreams and goals if God wants us to do something else for him? Does Christ really come *first* in all things? The cost of discipleship. It might mean the giving-up of our life, as Bonhoeffer did. Or it simply might mean doing something, no matter our age, out of our comfort zone; putting ourselves 'out there', to be used by God in some way. Jesus says: 'Follow me!' How will we respond?

Combating Corruption

All have turned aside, they have together become corrupt; there is no-one who does good, not even one (v. 3).

We live in a rather messed-up world. Of course, there is much good around us. But, when we look abroad, when we look at constant war, fighting, brutality – one against another – we soon see all the corruption that surrounds us. It's nothing new, as we can see from reading this psalm. Some people treat others in a way that's so hard to comprehend; as the psalmist says in the opening verse, deeds that are 'vile'. David goes to the extreme of saying that there is 'no-one' who does anything good – 'not even one'.

What, then, can we possibly do to combat all this corruption in the world? May I suggest several things we *can* do as Christians:

- *Pray*. Sometimes we don't pray enough for political leaders (especially the not-so-good ones). This is critical. Pray that they will have empathy, and will 'rule' with a true sense of justice.
- *Read Scripture*. We need to *hear* what God is saying to us through his Word. We must ask him to let us know how we can fight injustice and corruption in our world.
- *Fast*. Often this discipline enables us to hear from God, who then gives further insight and direction. If it's not a regular practice, try it from time to time. Even one meal a day. God will bless you for it.
- *Be involved*. It is important to be involved in our community, our neighbourhood, as much as possible. By doing this, people will hopefully see Christ in us.
- *Love*. Genuine love goes further than one could ever imagine. Let's love and be a refuge for others – especially the poor, the afflicted. With love, there is the possibility for peace.

Thought

Send a letter to one of your political leaders today, saying you're praying for them – asking that God will give them daily wisdom and guidance.

Our Father

'Our Father in heaven, hallowed be your name' (v. 9).

There is a beautiful rendition of the Lord's Prayer, to be sung, which begins as follows:

> Our Father, who in Heaven art, All hallowed be thy name,
> Thy Kingdom come to every heart To light the holy flame.
>
> (Charles Coller, *SASB* 624)

The Lord's Prayer is recited, or sung, in various languages around the world. In doing this, it honours God. Christ gave this prayer to his followers, yet it was also his prayer to *his* Father. In many countries today, it's Father's Day. A day to remember and honour fathers. Some do not have good memories of their father, or don't even know who their father is. So, for some, it's a difficult day.

My own father died very suddenly, nearly twenty years ago. Months after his death, I wrote a 'letter' to him. Perhaps an excerpt from this letter might resonate with someone else today:

> Dear Dad . . . Most people have memories of their fathers. Some are not good memories. For those I weep, for they have not known the joy of a rich father–child relationship. Yet those who believe in Jesus have the glorious anticipation of being with their Heavenly Father one day . . . Heaven has become very real to me because you are there. I'm confident in that blessed assurance! Dad, I miss you beyond words. Yet I promise to keep fighting in the war against sin and Satan, as you so faithfully did . . . One day, I'll see you again, and we'll see our Lord, together, face to face . . . With all my love . . .

Our earthly fathers – memories. Our Heavenly Father – the hope of eternal life! The song concludes with this verse, a prayer for us all:

> The kingdoms of the world are thine, Thine too the praise shall be;
> Grant us to worship at thy shrine To all eternity.

As for Me and My Family . . .

'But as for me and my family, we will serve the LORD' (v. 15, NLT).

Joshua speaks from his heart, for he knows he's close to death. He gets right to the point, holding nothing back:

'Choose today whom you will serve' (v. 15, NLT).

It was a challenge put out to the people; for the choice was theirs to make. Not for tomorrow, or the next year; but for *today*. They were to choose, today, whom they would serve. Joshua clearly had made his choice. No, he wasn't claiming perfection; he wasn't saying all his family members were perfect, never to go astray. He was simply saying he loved God, chose to serve him supremely, and would do everything in his power to encourage his family to do likewise.

What does this 'choosing' to serve the Lord involve? A right *motive*. We choose him because it's our deep desire to love and serve him. Our *destiny* is involved. The choice we make determines eternal life, or death. It involves our *well-being*. Choosing Christ affects our life journey. The right choice made gives us *hope*. It gives to us direction and purpose for life itself. We choose Christ because of *love*. He has such great love for us; we are to love him in return.

Joshua gathered his people at Shechem, recounting the outstanding events that had taken place in the lives of the children of Israel. The patriarchal days; the days of the Exodus; now, the conquest of the promised land. The good times; the difficult times.

We are all engaged in the amazing 'circle of life'. We are here to build on relationships; to live together in harmony, in community, as family. The dramatist W. S. Gilbert once said: 'It isn't so much what's on the table that matters as what's on the chairs.' We should always take time to build on our relationships, for they are essential for healthy living – our family, our friends.

Today, take time to share the fragrance of God's presence with those you love so dearly. For 'family', no matter what that word means to you, is so very precious indeed.

Prayer of Faith

'O LORD Almighty, if you will only look upon your servant's misery and remember me' (v. 11).

The two books of Samuel are actually only one book in the Hebrew manuscript; therefore, we will look at them together. They cover a range of nearly a hundred years – probably one of the most important centuries in the history of Israel. Again, this devotional material is not meant to be a commentary; rather, an overview of Scripture, an encouragement for daily living. For the God whose activity is being reported about in these two important books is the same God who works out his design for our lives today.

In this opening chapter we are introduced to a woman who is barren – a disgrace for people in her day. She no doubt must have felt like a spiritual leper, shunned by society. Yet Hannah had faith, strong enough to believe God would answer her prayer; a prayer she had made for years. We are told her husband, Elkanah, had two wives, which was permitted and accepted to a certain extent among the Israelites at that time. He seemed to have the one, Peninnah, for bearing children – both sons turning out to be corrupt. The other, Hannah, he loved deeply. Because of this love, Peninnah despised Hannah – mistreating her whenever possible.

Hannah felt abandoned by God, by others. Yet she still held on to her faith. She was even willing, if granted a child, to give him back to God; to miss out on raising him, seeing him go to school for the first time, seeing him play with other children. Yes; if God would grant her this precious gift, he would be used for God's service.

We all have dreams and desires for ourselves, for our children. Most of us want things from God. If God grants us the prayer of our heart, are we ready and willing to offer that gift back to him?

When we pray today, let's make sure our prayer is pure in motive, and unselfish in its intent. What are we asking God for this day?

Prayer

Lord, may my heart's desire be only for your ultimate glory!

Prayer of Rejoicing

Then Hannah prayed and said: 'My heart rejoices in the Lord' (v. 1).

The Lord answered Hannah's prayer. God gave to her a beautiful baby boy, Samuel. After nursing him, she wanted to fulfil her promise to God. She bundled him up and brought him to the high priest, Eli, for service in God's house. It must have been very difficult for her, giving over her little son – the son she'd longed for, for so many years. Yet she knew it was something that must take place; for her heart was still full of rejoicing over God's faithfulness:

'There is no-one holy like the Lord; there is no-one besides you; there is no Rock like our God' (v. 2).

Hannah could only give praise and thanksgiving; for it was a time of rejoicing for her. Thus she sang a psalm, or song, to her Lord. We don't know the tune; but perhaps, as we recite these verses, we can make up one, singing with her from the heart – identifying *our* thanks to God for something wonderful he has done for *us*.

'He raises the poor from the dust and lifts the needy from the ash heap; he seats them with princes and has them inherit a throne of honour' (v. 8).

Most of us are not wealthy. Yet by relative standards, many of us are. Brothers and sisters in various parts of the world have little by comparison; yet the prayer indicates that one day they'll be lifted up, receiving a place of honour! God is just, seeing beginning to end. Because of this we can also offer a prayer of rejoicing, for:

'It is not by strength that one prevails' (v. 9).

It's not the wealthy, the powerful, the famous who win in the end; it's the one who desires only to serve the Lord.

Let's sing a song of rejoicing to our Father, praising him for what he has done for us, through us, in us. As with Hannah, may it be our humble offering and act of worship this day.

The Mustard Seed

'The kingdom of heaven is like a mustard seed' (v. 31).

Jesus was a wonderful story-teller. He used parables – short stories, told to convey one basic point. When interpreting them, we should always look for that one point, and not try to hang truths based on every detail of the story as though they were allegorical. Also we must always consider the culture, language and context of the day in which they were told. A parable was to be heard, not analysed and dissected on manuscript. For Jesus was interested in the real life of people, wanting them to 'seek first' the kingdom of God in all they did. He wants the same for us today.

Matthew 13 contains seven of these parables, all concerning the kingdom of heaven. These particular parables are those of assurance, whereas parables found elsewhere are often parables of the gospel, or of the *parusia* (second coming). One of these seven speaks of the mustard seed – found also in Mark and Luke. Here, a man deliberately plants this very small seed in his field. Even though it's an insignificant beginning, this tiny seed eventually grows into a plant or tree over twelve feet high – tall enough for birds to find a resting place on its many branches.

The parable tells us that the kingdom of God grows, becoming a place of rest and shade; a place of stability and peace. It becomes the greater expression of the sower's purposive activity. This same kingdom grows to inevitably achieve wonderful results for so many needing Christ's love and care and protection.

Several chapters later, Jesus refers again to this tiny mustard seed (17:20). Even though our faith might be very small, even possibly wavering somewhat, this tiny bit of faith we may possess can grow to the point of telling a mountain to move! For, as Jesus concludes:

'Nothing will be impossible for you' (17:21).

The mustard seed: Protection. Assurance. Faith. Love. God's presence. Yes, all things *are* indeed possible – in Christ!

Extravagant Love

'She has done a beautiful thing to me' (v. 10).

It was an act of worship. While the religious leaders were busy plotting against Jesus, his friends gathered together in Bethany with their Lord, to show their love and devotion.

The feast took place six days before the Passover, as recorded in John 12:1, in the house of a man known as Simon the Leper – a man who had been healed by Jesus. Picture the setting: Simon the host, Mary, Martha, Lazarus, Judas and Jesus – along with other guests. Only John identifies the woman with the alabaster jar of perfume as Mary. She is at Jesus' feet; deeply spiritual, deeply devoted.

Mary takes the perfume – perfume that cost roughly a whole year's wages – and anoints both Jesus' head and feet with it. She then proceeds to wipe his feet with her hair, a woman's glory. In doing this, she is surrendering her glory to the Lord in worship, in love, in adoration. The whole house becomes filled with its fragrance.

She's immediately criticised for this act by none other than Judas. He thinks the money the perfume was worth should have been put to a much better use. But his motives are not pure in saying this. She shows extravagant love. She gives all she has for her Saviour. Judas, and perhaps others with him, are no doubt jealous and envious of her act. She's misunderstood. Only Jesus sees her sacrificial act as being beautiful.

Mary gives from the heart. It costs her a lot of money. But that is not even a question nor an issue for her. And then, the fragrance of this lovely act of devotion and worship lingers on. In fact it still lingers with us, even now.

Here we are today, two thousand years later, reading of this beautiful account. And so we ask ourselves: What can we do that will be our act of worship today – something that will show our extravagant love for Jesus Christ? What can we do to create a fragrance that will be both beautiful and honouring to our Lord? Let's think about this; pray about it – then, let's act accordingly.

Pure and Holy Living

Listen well to my words of insight, that you may maintain discretion and your lips may preserve knowledge (vv. 1, 2).

Several chapters in the book of Proverbs set out warnings against adultery. It was a prevalent issue then – and nothing has changed. It's interesting that these same proverbs are attributed to King Solomon, who had more than one thousand wives and concubines!

May you rejoice in the wife of your youth (v. 18).

In other words, you fell in love once and married. Be satisfied in that relationship. 'Maintain discretion' with any others. Be careful in other interactions with people, not wanting a physical attraction to develop inappropriately. Rather, we're to enhance the relationship we already have with our wife or husband:

May you ever be captivated by her [his] love (v. 19).

One would think this is how most marriages work, especially Christian marriages. According to statistics this is not necessarily true. Oh, couples may stay together in the marriage due to cultural pressure. But many marriages are not *faithful* marriages. Adultery creeps into all cultures. Love, commitment and fidelity have disintegrated in many instances. And everyone suffers.

What's the answer? Pure and holy living. Simple; yet hard to embrace by many. Faithfulness within a marriage context takes discipline, commitment and love. It takes a total devotion to one's partner and to God. For God even knows our thought-life:

For a man's ways are in full view of the LORD, and he examines all his paths (v. 21).

Today, do something special for your spouse. If not married, or your spouse has passed on before you, write an encouraging note to a married couple. Pray that *all* will live pure and holy lives.

Don't Assume

'I will heal their waywardness and love them freely' (v. 4).

The words of this song come from a Salvation Army musical, *Hosea*:

> Don't assume that God's dismissed you from his mind,
> Don't assume that God's forgotten to be kind;
> For no matter what you do, his love still follows you;
> Don't think that you have left him far behind.
>
> (John Gowans, *SASB* 44)

Do you ever feel God has forgotten you? Or that you've messed up so badly, he won't want to have anything to do with you? Maybe you've neglected God for a period of time; and since you have felt him rather unimportant in your life, perhaps you think he's felt the same way about you. Most of us have gone through some of these feelings, or even a mixture of them, at one point or another.

The context from which this song arises, and even the whole musical itself, is a powerful one. The prophet Hosea was asked by God to take a prostitute – Gomer – to be his wife. He does so; then Gomer cheats on him. He's asked to take her back. In the musical, this is happening in the life of the man playing the part of Hosea. A play within a play. Tragedy, all around. He's a broken husband, struggling to raise three children. As a man of God, he wants to be obedient. He's only able to do this because he trusts God implicitly.

God instructs Hosea to speak to the Israelites, who have turned from him. Another layer to the story. God was faithful; he wanted faithfulness in return. Why should they trust him? The refrain sums it up – for us all:

> For his love remains the same, he knows you by your name,
> Don't think because you've failed him he despairs;
> For he gives to those who ask his grace for every task,
> God plans for you in love for he still cares.

Are you assured of his unconditional love today?

Listening

'Speak, LORD, for your servant is listening' (v. 9).

L istening is a learned skill. We all can 'listen'; but do we always *hear* what
is being said? There are many voices clamouring to be heard. Some voices
are not good at all. It boils down to listening *well*. What is God saying to us,
as we set out to live for him?

Most of us know well the story of Samuel's calling. He was probably
around twelve years of age, living under the mentorship of Eli. It was this
same Eli who had spent so much time doing God's work, to the detriment of
his own family life. His sons had let God down, big time. He was determined
to do better by Samuel.

It's interesting to note the opening of this chapter:

In those days the word of the LORD was rare (v. 1).

We can gather from this statement that there was an atmosphere of spiritual
apathy in the land. Perhaps there were definitive places where people gathered
to worship out of habit; perhaps the people even called themselves people of
faith. Yet one can be *religious* without being spiritually alive and in tune with
God; a 'believer' without really having a desire to listen closely to God's
voice.

But one night Samuel clearly heard a voice. Thinking it was Eli, he went to
the priest, saying he was ready to do as requested. He was obedient, listened
well, and responded accordingly. After the third time, Eli caught on to what
was happening. He proceeded to awaken Samuel's spiritual perception, so
that the young boy would understand that Jehovah God wanted to speak to
him personally. Samuel then returned to his room, ready to really listen.

We've *all* been called by God; and God often speaks to us through familiar
voices. It might be an Eli or a family member; it might be through Scripture or
prayer. God might use *us* to speak to a Samuel. All he wants us to keep on
saying, as we listen to him, is:

'Here I am' (v. 16).

The Pursuit of Happiness

She named the boy Ichabod, saying, 'The glory has departed from Israel'
(v. 21).

Do you recall ever seeing bright yellow buttons with smiley faces on them?
The happy-face symbol was actually created in 1963 by graphic artist
Harvey Ross Ball, who was asked by his employer to create a logo that would
encourage employees to smile as they went about their work. That smiley face
became an icon, worldwide, for an entire generation. At its peak in 1971,
more than fifty million smiley-face buttons were sold.

Even though the buttons are seldom seen now, the pursuit of happiness has
always been with us. Then one can ask: Who is really happy – the rich, the
famous? Apparently it has nothing much to do with wealth or status.

According to the North American *Forbes* magazine, a recent survey
indicated that the 400 richest people in the world might seem happy, but are
no more so than the Masai of East Africa – who have no electricity and are
living in dung huts. It's all about what's going on *inside*; about motivation,
reason for living, purpose, spiritual integrity, awareness of God's presence.

The portion of Scripture for today tells us the Israelites went out to fight
the Philistines. They wanted to be happy, claiming territory for themselves.
However, they had been selfish in their pursuit of happiness by doing this in
their own strength, in their own way.

The ark of the covenant, symbolising God's presence, was brought into the
camp; but surrounding it were Hophni and Phinehas – Eli's sons – who had
abandoned God for their own selfish desires. The Philistines fought and
defeated them; in so doing, they captured the ark. The two brothers were
killed in battle. Eli died of a broken neck – and a broken heart; and the nation
itself was broken. Phinehas's wife gave birth to a son, Ichabod, indicating that
the glory of God had departed from them.

A true and deep sense of happiness comes only from having faith affirmed
and restored. Inner peace, joy and happiness occur when we're in a right
relationship with the Almighty. Let us, today, bask in God's great love and be
truly happy – in him.

Rhythms of Grace

'They have rejected me as their king' (v. 7).

Samuel soon became a judge in Israel. But the Israelites looked around, seeing that other nations had kings to rule, not mere judges. They wanted to be known as powerful; a nation to be feared, revered and recognised worldwide. They wanted a king of their own, an *earthly* king.

So often we think we know what's best. We might even have fairly good intentions, being engaged in God's work. We press forward making our own decisions, hoping God will eventually bless our efforts when we're done. We think we have it all together. There's a beautiful verse in the Gospel of Matthew, chapter 11, taken from *The Message* paraphrase:

Learn the unforced rhythms of grace (v. 29).

God designed a divine rhythm to life. For creation – night, day; work, rest; winter, spring. But also for his children and our day-to-day life: a time to move forward, then to hold back; a time to speak, and a time to listen. Only God sees beginning to end. Only God knows the specific rhythm he so desires for each life. This is why we must trust him, for *all* things.

God had a specific plan for the Israelites. He, alone, wanted to be their leader, their king. But they couldn't trust him for this. They wanted to take their own direction. Prestige and recognition were far more important to them. Thus, they desperately tried to squeeze him out of their lives. For they knew best.

When we embrace the rhythms of his grace, we will live a balanced life; one that is healthy emotionally, physically, spiritually. For we will be trusting God with rhythms that are perfect for *you*, for me.

Prayer

Lord, help me to be completely free in the beautiful rhythms of your grace today. Help me affirm my allegiance to you as Lord and King of my life.

His Finished Work

Then they led him away to crucify him (v. 31).

No matter how many times we read the Passion story, we're still touched and deeply moved. First, Christ being arrested and tried by the Jews, then also by the Romans. The scourging, the pain, the agony, the eventual death. Yes, the cross, and all its implications, has been referred to by some as the 'fulcrum' of cosmic history. For the eternal destiny of every human being hinges on a person's relationship with Christ and the work he did on the cross for all.

When we think of family, friends, our neighbourhoods, our cities, we soon come to realise that so many have not come to the cross in faith, receiving salvation. Many do not have that assurance of eternal life, all because of the finished work of Christ on the cross. What, then, can we do to help point others to Calvary today?

It might mean writing a letter to someone. Perhaps it's a family member. We've been putting this off, unsure of how it will be received. It might mean giving a Bible, or a devotional book, to someone. Maybe it's a phone call we need to make, or an email to be sent. It might mean a visit to see or meet up with someone.

We're not alone when we do these things – if we ask for God's Spirit to be with us. For we need to say the right words, in the way God would have us do. To ask for his direction, his leading; to share the gospel of Christ in the right way in order that a life will be changed, forever.

Jesus died. His work was finished on the cross. The tomb where he was buried made the death official. But then, the victory! The angel tells the women on that first day of the week:

'He has risen from the dead' (Matthew 28:7).

Christ's resurrection is the ultimate event in Christology; for in the resurrection, his ministry is forever confirmed – inaugurating the kingdom of God. There is no greater news to be told! Who will you share this transforming revelation with today?

The Great Commission

'Therefore go and make disciples of all nations' (v. 19).

J esus states that all authority, all *exousia*, had been given to him, in heaven
and on earth. This is a declaration of the ultimate victory on the cross. And
under this same supreme authority, the disciples were to go and share Christ
– the Christian message, the hope of salvation, the promise of eternal life –
with the whole world. As believers, two thousand years later, we also share in
this Great Commission, having this same authority given to us. Not only to
tell the news, but to 'make disciples'.

A disciple is more than a convert. A disciple is an 'apprentice', one who
learns from another; who learns by listening, then doing. We ourselves have
been discipled by others. And so we, in turn, are to *make disciples*. Then *they*
can go out and do likewise.

It's not all up to the ministers of the congregation. The Great Commission
is for *all* – no matter where we find ourselves in life. But how do we do this
effectively? Jesus concludes:

'I am with you always, to the very end of the age' (v. 20).

Around the world, even today as people read this in North or South America,
in Europe or Asia or Africa, we are assured that Christ is *with* us. He connects
us to one another, as we reach out to a world in desperate need of Christ. He
tells us that one day everything will come to an end. But until then, we're to
be faithful – fulfilling the Great Commission as his committed disciples.

What a privilege is ours, to share Christ with others! Then, when we're
frightened or nervous, or even timid, we are to remember that he is with us
– *always*.

Prayer

Today, O Lord, may I prove to be a faithful disciple, as I carry forth the Great
Commission – into the nation, the community, you've given to me. May
people be receptive and open to your presence.

Entering into Worship

LORD, who may dwell in your sanctuary? (v. 1).

Have you ever run into a worship service somewhat frazzled? Have you ever sat down to have your devotional time, overwhelmed with all you have to get done that day? Have you ever tried to come into God's presence when you have just had a harsh word with someone? Have you ever approached worshipping God having just done something not right?

I have. And it's a terrible experience. There can almost be a sense of phoniness, or hypocrisy, about it. Yes, it's better to *try* and sense God's presence; attending church is probably better than staying at home. But when one's mind, one's heart, is somewhere else, the distance you set apart from God's heart can be very disturbing.

God still wants us to come to him when we're upset. He still wants us to be in conversation with him when our emotions are out of whack. But he then quickly wants us to lay it all before him, asking for forgiveness, seeking his presence, making amends with others. Who, then, is *worthy* to enter into worship?

He whose walk is blameless and who does what is righteous, who speaks the truth from his heart (v. 2).

We're to have a heart that desires to make things right with God, and with others. This is how we are to enter worship. We're to care for one another, for we are brothers and sisters in Christ. We're Christ's light in a dark world. We're to uphold one another, support, encourage one another. When we enter into worship with the right kind of attitude, with our eyes fixed on Christ, what then happens?

He [she] who does these things will never be shaken (v. 5).

May we enter into worship, today, with a humble and contrite heart. May we enter into worship, filled with love for our Lord.

My Jesus, I Love Thee

'My unfailing love for you will not be shaken' (v. 10).

Today's song is a beautiful love song to Jesus. It's intimate, personal; it speaks of commitment, loyalty; it reflects the deepest of emotions. It's a response to God's love toward us. So often we don't know how to express our most profound feelings for him. This song does it for us. How much do we love him? Let's count the ways! We love him enough to give up sin – striving for a life of holiness:

> My Jesus, I love thee, I know thou art mine,
> For thee all the pleasures of sin I resign.
> (William Ralph Featherstone, *SASB* 357)

The world tells me to indulge, enjoy, live it up. But I *can* enjoy life, fully, *without* sin – for Jesus is my Saviour and Lord. Why do I love him so much? Because he loves me – proving it by dying on the cross:

> I love thee because thou hast first lovèd me,
> And purchased my pardon on Calvary's tree. (v. 2)

I love him today, and will continue to love him until I die. He has transformed me, giving me purpose, and a reason for living:

> I will love thee in life, I will love thee in death,
> And praise thee as long as thou lendest me breath. (v. 3)

This is *my* love song to Jesus – from my heart, to his. He's my light, my song, my very breath; he's my all in all – for now, for always:

> In mansions of glory and endless delight,
> I'll ever adore thee and dwell in thy sight;
> I'll sing with the glittering crown on my brow:
> If ever I loved thee, my Jesus, 'tis now! (v. 4)

Firsts

Then Samuel took a flask of oil and poured it on Saul's head and kissed him (v. 1).

The Lord told Samuel to give the Israelites what they wanted, a king. It was to be their *first* king. They desperately wanted to be a nation that was recognised. With this new king, they would set themselves on a new adventure of excitement and glory.

Firsts. Think back to a few 'firsts' in your life. Your first day at school, or that first crush on a girl or boy. Maybe think about your first job, that first pay cheque. These *firsts* are sometimes scary; but the adrenaline soon kicks in.

Much that follows that 'first' experience depends upon how we are treated and how we react. Even our first encounter with sickness or even death can be quite traumatic. So much has to do with who's with us and how we work it through.

The most important event in our life is that very first encounter with Christ. Perhaps it occurred when we were young, or maybe as an adult. Did we immediately want to know him more, and better? Are we just as excited today about our life with Christ as we were then? Even more so?

This was a *first* for the Israelites – a king. They wanted to be first – when it came to power and prestige and fame. Their motive was not in the right place. Yet God granted their desire. But he knew what would happen when they chose an earthly king over a heavenly one.

Firsts. The very *first* thing we should do today is to commit it, entirely, to the Lord. Then tell him that he is, above all, *first* in our life. When we do this, everything else will fall into place – according to his design and will.

Prayer

Lord, I want to say to you today that I love you – so very much! Help this thought permeate all I say and do this day. I am yours, *totally*.

'Climate' Change

'You have not kept the LORD's command' (v. 14).

There is much talk today about global warming and climate change. Flooding, for example, seems to be happening in so many places worldwide – with devastating outcomes. Governments look at cyclical weather patterns as the root cause, rather than tackling the whole area of environmental issues. They do this at their own peril, and at the expense of future generations.

Just as there is talk of environmental climate change, there can also be 'climate change' when it comes to relationships. In Israel, Saul had been chosen as king. But before long he began taking things into his own hands. The Philistines were gathering their army together, ready to go to battle against the Israelites. Saul had been warned to wait for Samuel to come, so he could offer a sacrifice to the Lord – as with any battle. Samuel was delayed; so Saul made the sacrifice himself. He was impatient.

With this act of disobedience against God, the *climate*, the atmosphere, changed for Saul. Samuel eventually arrived, saw what Saul had done, then had to relay the message God gave to him: Saul would no longer be king. He would lose God's blessing. The Israelites would be defeated.

When we do things our own way, everyone loses. Here we see the conflict and disagreement between Saul and Samuel, two leaders – broken relationships. We also see that Saul's independent action laid the foundation for his failure as king – broken man. We know, too, that he disobeyed God – broken covenant:

'You have not kept the command the LORD your God gave you' (v. 13).

Today, let's pause to pray for those affected by climate change and natural disaster; then let's make sure we pause to pray for our continual relationships with others – that they be holy and right before God.

Consequences

'Now I beg you, forgive my sin and come back with me, so that I may worship the LORD' (v. 25).

With sin comes consequence. We all sin; and when it happens, there must be repentance. The forgiveness we then receive is because of God's mercy and his grace. But there are consequences that come – some more severe than others.

Saul realised he'd sinned; but he minimised its seriousness. He soon began making excuses, reasons for his actions. He tried to somehow justify his sin. Saul thought both Samuel and God would simply forgive, then forget. He was shocked that Samuel wouldn't travel with him and even grabbed his robe, which tore. Samuel immediately used his torn robe as a symbol for Saul, to stress the point in the severity of his action:

'The LORD has torn the kingdom of Israel from you today' (v. 28).

Then, a very sad verse is recorded for us:

The LORD was grieved that he had made Saul king over Israel (v. 35).

Yes, a sad day for Israel, because their king had let them down. But a dreadful day for Saul, since God had rejected him as king – to the point of *grieving* that he'd ever made him king. And from what we know of his life, Saul never changed within.

Often we fail in talking much about sin. We speak of making 'mistakes' or 'slipping up'. But sin is very real, and very present in our world today. When we do sin, there are usually repercussions – and huge consequences.

Let's make sure *all* sin has been confessed before God. Then, even though we still may be living with the consequences of past and forgiven sin, let's bring this to the Lord – ensuring that we are living according to his perfect will.

The Word Became Flesh

In the beginning was the Word . . . The Word became flesh and made his dwelling among us (vv. 1, 14).

When we read the opening verse of John's Gospel, we immediately think back to the opening verse of Genesis. Yet here it is slightly different: *In the beginning was the Word* – or the *Logos* in Greek. What is the significance?

Logos signifies the outward form by which the inward thinking is expressed. In other words, to both think and speak out a specific thought. Thus, we have the Absolute and only God speaking, manifesting himself to the world. The *Logos* uttered; Christ, being the mediator between God and the world; *Logos*, who always was, and now is, and will always be.

When we see John referring to the *Word* in reference to Christ, we know he's speaking of a personal God. We think of a voice – God's voice speaking forth to his children, then and now. And this *Word* actually became flesh, in the very person of Jesus Christ. He was the revelation of God to the world. God incarnate.

In this profound 'prologue' to John's Gospel, the writer wants to identify the 'Messenger' of this good news to the world. And the startling information he gives is this: the Message and the Messenger are one and the same!

This extraordinary news of the Word becoming flesh contains four basic truths. First, the Word has always been with God as a distinct Person. Second, the mission of the Word is to enable people to have everlasting life. Third, this same mission of the Word is both successful and unsuccessful – depending upon the response it evokes. And fourth, the Word is historical fact – an identifiable human being, Jesus Christ; fully divine, fully human.

All glory be to him!

Lamb of God

'Look, the Lamb of God, who takes away the sin of the world!' (v. 29).

John the Baptist disclaimed being the Christ, when the Jewish priests and Levites questioned him. But he was also quick to announce that One would come who would exceed all Jewish baptisms; for he would baptise with the Holy Spirit. Yes, the One to come was far more worthy than John could ever be.

The very next day, John looked up – and there he was. John spoke, identifying to all 'the Lamb of God'. The Messiah had come! John used this title to speak of the sacrificial character of Christ's mission. It's a reflection of the prophesy in Isaiah:

He was led like a lamb to the slaughter (Isaiah 53:7).

Jesus, the Lamb of God, came to take away the sin of the world. It speaks to Jesus' atoning ministry and ultimate death. The promised Messiah had come; and with his death and resurrection we are all able to be forgiven and redeemed.

But something else happened that day. John affirmed the ministry of the Holy Spirit. The Holy Spirit both authenticated the mission of Jesus and was the seal of Christ's work in people's lives:

'The man on whom you see the Spirit come down and remain is he who will baptise with the Holy Spirit' (John 1:33).

Because of John's declaration of Jesus as the Lamb of God, and his affirmation of the Holy Spirit's presence, John's disciples left him to follow Jesus. The time had come. Our mission is also to announce that Christ is alive and present in our world; to tell others that the Lamb of God has made the supreme sacrifice for each one of us, and the Holy Spirit is wanting to dwell within each life. Yes, we too testify:

'This is the Son of God' (v. 34).

Prayer

Lamb of God, help me to always follow you; and help me to encourage others to follow you. For when they do, their destiny will be changed for eternity!

Path, Presence, Pleasures

You have made known to me the path of life; you will fill me with joy in your presence, with eternal pleasures at your right hand (v. 11).

Everyone needs to feel secure and safe. When something or someone threatens our security, the equilibrium is thrown off balance. This is when we cry out for divine protection:

Keep me safe, O God (v. 1).

Once we do feel safe, protected and secure – physically, emotionally, spiritually – it's then that we can become more aware of God: the *path* he has set for us, embracing his *presence* fully, and taking *pleasure* in his many blessings for us.

Yes, the *path* God sets out is very different for each one of us. Life's a journey, filled with both wonderful times and challenging times. When things are going smoothly, we thank God. Yet when the more difficult times come, we still have the assurance that there's a safe place in Christ; security in knowing he walks the path with us.

Our God is personal; one who makes his *presence* known to us. The psalmist reminds us that God's presence brings great joy. This same joy carries us into all we do in his name. Mother Teresa was once asked what was needed to work in the alleys of Calcutta. Her answer? 'The desire to work hard, with a joyful attitude.' Joy, because God's presence is so very real.

God also promises us eternal *pleasures*, an abundance of blessings. If we seek refuge, safety, security in him, he will reward us with pleasures beyond our imagination: the pleasure of an eternal 'inheritance' (v. 6); the pleasure of knowing that our 'lot' in life is secure with Christ; the pleasure of knowing we'll be resurrected.

The *path*; his *presence*; the *pleasures*. Oh yes; with this kind of affirmation we can declare:

'You are my Lord' (v. 2).

Holy, Holy, Holy

Day and night they never stop saying: 'Holy, holy, holy is the Lord God Almighty, who was, and is, and is to come' (v. 8).

If ever there was a hymn to bring us into the majestic presence of the Lord our God, first thing in the morning, it is this one:

> Holy, holy, holy, Lord God Almighty!
> Early in the morning our song shall rise to thee;
> Holy, holy, holy, merciful and mighty,
> God in three persons, blessèd Trinity!
> (Reginald Heber, *SASB* 220)

This hymn brings us to the throne of God – everyone present casting down 'crowns' and bowing before him:

> Cherubim and seraphim falling down before thee,
> Who wert, and art, and evermore shalt be! (v. 2)

We're reminded in this powerful hymn of sin in the world – in contrast with a God who is pure, sinless, perfect, holy. He's not a God who is full of revenge; but one who is filled with mercy – all because of his love for us:

> Only thou art holy; there is none beside thee
> Perfect in power, in love and purity! (v. 3)

Will you commence this day by singing this last verse with me? For it reminds us that *all* should be praising God for who he is:

> Holy, holy, holy, Lord God Almighty!
> All thy works shall praise thy name in earth and sky and sea;
> Holy, holy, holy, merciful and mighty,
> God in three persons, blessèd Trinity! (v. 4)

The Heart

'The LORD does not see as man sees; men judge by appearances but the LORD judges by the heart' (v. 7, NEB).

This is perhaps one of the most important verses in all of Scripture. It was in seeming contrast with the culture of the day. Appearances were so very important. It's also in contradiction with most cultures today; for people look at the *outside* of a person: their appearance, their status, their credentials. Yet it clearly states that God is looking not at these things, but rather at what's going on inside; looking at the inner person. He's looking at the *heart*.

God continually makes choices that surprise us. Being human, we think we know what's best: who should be the leader of our church – internationally, nationally, locally. We think we know who should be called into ministry, or who should lead different sections of our church. But ultimately, it's God's choice. He knows what's in the heart of people – their motivation, their sincerity, their integrity, their devotion to and love for God.

Although Samuel was no doubt surprised that God had chosen young David – ruddy in complexion, a shepherd boy – if this was who God had chosen to be the next king of Israel, then he would anoint him. And what came next?

From that day on the Spirit of the LORD came upon David in power (v. 13).

David was empowered, by God's Spirit, to do the great task that lay before him. It's no different today. When God chooses us, he empowers us – creating in us such joy, love and peace.

Prayer

Lord, I love you with all my *heart*. May this same heart remain pure and given only to you. And may I extend this love to others so that they, too, will know of your majesty, power and grace.

Giants and Battles

'The whole world will know that there is a God' (v. 46).

In many cultures today we tend to cheer for the underdog, for it's somehow great to see a 'nobody' overcome a *giant*. The story of David and Goliath is this kind of story. Yet it's also so much more. It's about the people of God fighting against people and things *not* of God. The word 'defy' is mentioned. The Philistines – the giant – *defied* the living God. This was not to be tolerated.

On a corporate level Christians today, similar to the Israelites years ago, are under attack. Great battles are taking place. There's the *intellectual* battle – the world trying to tell Christians they're weak-minded, intellectually inferior. They're told they need to expand their minds, be exposed to other philosophies. The battle continues.

There's also the *moral* battle for righteousness. Things have changed. We live in an era that no longer craves for goodness and godliness. People have become passive, seemingly accepting of things that are morally corrupt. The battle continues.

On a personal level, many are fighting demons within; struggles that are fierce. These 'giants' tend to consume people, for they face them daily. Perhaps they're addictions; perhaps deep conflicts within. The 'giant' calls out, mocking, jeering; and with it comes constant defeat, and the agony that follows.

Whether it's a corporate battle, or a deeply personal one, the eventual 'contest' must take place. One has to face the giant in battle. Who will win? It's up to us, really.

Today, if there are giants we're facing, battles that need to be won, we must take them to the Lord and trust him implicitly with the outcome. Then we must also pray for others, that victory will be theirs.

Jealousy

And from that time on Saul kept a jealous eye on David (v. 9).

The unanimous love of the people for David drove a wedge between Saul and his faithful servant. The women would come out from the cities, after a battle had been won, singing and dancing – chanting the same verse, over and over, again and again:

'Saul has slain his thousands, and David his tens of thousands' (v. 7).

It drove Saul mad; an arrow straight into his heart. He was full of rage – and extreme jealousy. Saul even tried to kill David, twice. But the deeper issue was Saul's awareness that the Lord was with David, and had departed from him. How very sad.

Jealousy can consume a person. Being jealous of another person can zap every ounce of energy from within. Perhaps it's jealousy of another's looks, status, the way they're treated by others. We envy them; and we start to have awful feelings about them.

It's what we *do* with these feelings that's crucial. It's how we handle the jealous thoughts and emotions. And yes, it rears its ugly head in Christian circles, all too frequently. We see someone more popular with others; someone with a great talent being used, admired by all; someone promoted, while we're working so hard.

Jealousy can fester. It can take over our thought-life. It can eat away at our very soul. When the feeling comes, we must be set free – before it ensnares us. And this can only be done by God himself.

Prayer

God, take any jealous thoughts away from me, so I can live freely in your great love. Thank you for those who have many gifts and talents. Use them for your glory; and help me to grow to be more like your Son, Jesus Christ – day by day.

God so Loved

'Whoever lives by the truth comes into the light, so that it may be seen plainly that what he has done has been done through God' (v. 21).

The verse many of us have memorised since childhood is the most important message of John's Gospel:

'For God so loved the world that he gave his one and only Son, that whoever believes in him shall not perish but have eternal life' (v. 16).

Salvation is a gift, received only by believing in Jesus. The result of our belief is eternal life – free from condemnation. It's about being in a relationship of total honesty with God. If we accept Christ, we will not 'perish'; for when something perishes it is lost, destroyed. If someone doesn't accept God's love, they are excluded from fellowship with him. So, there are only two options: to believe or to perish. To live freely, eternally; or to exist with utter failure, futility and eternal loss.

God wants *no one* to perish. This is why he sent his Son:

'To save the world through him' (v. 17).

It's about our attitude toward the 'light'. Light exposes sin. We need complete transparency before God; complete honesty before the Creator. The plan of salvation has been set – rooted in God's love.

It is God who has taken the initiative. He's made the necessary provisions and has paid the debt. He then waits for a response. It's all about the will – the *free will* that God has given to each of us. We can respond positively to the magnetic power and love of Christ, or repel him. It's then about faith; to believe, and accept, this wonderful good news.

Thought

We all have family and friends who have rejected Christ. Make contact with someone today, and share the 'light' you've experienced with them.

Death to Life

'I tell you the truth, whoever hears my word and believes him who sent me has eternal life and will not be condemned; he has crossed over from death to life' (v. 24).

People tend to be more casual about faith today. They might claim to be spiritual; they might even say they believe in God. But when you speak of accepting Christ as their personal Saviour, they may say they're not ready – or willing – to take this step.

The Jews caught Jesus performing a miracle on the Sabbath. After healing a paralysed man, they questioned him about doing 'work' on this sacred day. Jesus went on to claim he was God's Son. This was blasphemy to the Jews. Yet Jesus responded by saying those who *believed* in him would cross over from death to life.

Many people become obsessed with death – or the avoidance of it. Researchers are desperately striving to discover ways to prolong life for as long as possible. Apparently the human body peaks at age twenty-five. A hundred years ago, this was roughly middle age for most people worldwide. Although we're living much longer, our bodies still peak at the same age. We're now just 'extending' the timeline on the other end. It's not only the deterioration of the body that is the main issue as we get older; it's the deterioration of the senses and the failing of the mind.

Nothing can prevent the inevitable. But the wonderful news is this: Jesus Christ offers a place for us once we leave this life. He offers us everlasting life:

'Those who hear will live' (v. 25).

We're to have no fear of death. It's merely a stepping stone to a new and exciting life, which begins once we accept Christ. Death to life. What better news to share with the world?

Prayer

Father, help me to reach out to someone today, someone fearing death. May your Spirit speak through me, giving them reassurance of eternal *life* ahead – if they trust in God completely.

The Apple of Your Eye

Keep me as the apple of your eye; hide me in the shadow of your wings (v. 8).

L ord, I want to be the apple of your eye! It's a lot to ask for; and I really don't deserve anything at all. But it's such a beautiful image – and it would mean the world to me!

I remember, Father, each of my children, the day they were born. I looked at their little faces – so innocent, sweet, precious – and I whispered: 'My sweet little baby, you're the apple of my eye!' Each was given to me, from you, as a gift. I'm filled with such emotion just thinking back to those moments. Then, to watch them all grow to love you as young adults.

In this same way, and yet even in a more profound way, I want to be the apple of *your* eye, my Lord! You know I've messed up along the journey; I'm so far from perfection. To be honest, God, sometimes I really wonder what I'm doing to bring you honour and glory. I do acts of service; I pray and read Scripture; I try not to sin. But am I really doing enough? Is my whole body, mind, spirit, given *fully* to you? Can I *ever*, really, be the apple of your eye?

I just read the verse again. It says, 'Keep me . . .' I never really noticed this before, Lord. It says to me that I *am* the apple of your eye already! I'm completely yours, and you're pleased with me! Even with my faults, my shortcomings, you are there for me – hiding me 'in the shadow of your wings'.

It astounds me, baffles me, Lord. But I go forth in the assurance that I'm genuinely and truly loved – because I'm the apple of your eye!

Thought

Share with someone today the assurance that they're the apple of God's eye. Share the Scripture verse as well. Celebrate, with them, in this beautiful affirmation!

Take Time to be Holy

'Be holy, because I am holy' (v. 16).

> Take time to be holy, speak oft with thy Lord;
> Abide in him always, and feed on his word;
> Make friends of God's children; help those who are weak;
> Forgetting in nothing his blessing to seek.
>
> *(SASB 458)*

The words to this hymn were written in 1882 by William D. Longstaff, after hearing a sermon based on our text for today. Taking time. It's not easy, is it? Time is such a precious commodity. Time to work effectively, time to study and read. Also, time for developing friendships in our fast-paced, technologically advanced world; time with family, time for self. We need to 'Take time to be holy' for 'the world rushes on' (v. 2).

But have we ever really stopped to think about taking time to be *holy*? The Salvation Army is a holiness movement. The Church at large needs to embrace a new sense of *holiness*. But taking 'time to be holy'? Doesn't holiness just come to Christians? Verse 2 continues:

> Spend much time in secret with Jesus alone;
> By looking to Jesus, like him thou shalt be.

We're to intentionally spend time 'in secret', in communion with Jesus. We're not to rush ahead with our own agenda; but rather, to stop. When we take time to dwell in his presence, our 'thought' process and motive *becomes* holy. We're then ready for service – here, and in glory!

> Take time to be holy, be calm in thy soul;
> Each thought and each motive beneath his control;
> Thus led by his Spirit to fountains of love,
> Thou soon shalt be fitted for service above. (v. 4)

Friendship and Fellowship

'Go in peace, for we have sworn friendship with each other in the name of the LORD' (v. 42).

David depended upon the Lord. And because of this, God helped him become skilled in what he did. He soon became very popular. But he faced many problems when it came to King Saul. For the king was soon made aware of David's popularity among the people. Therefore, Saul was becoming more difficult and dangerous, seeking out David's life.

David desperately needed a confidante. God provided one in Saul's eldest son, Jonathan. They were soul brothers, sharing in rich fellowship. In fact, Scripture says:

Jonathan became one in spirit with David, and he loved him as himself (1 Samuel 18:1).

The literal translation really means that the soul of Jonathan was *chained* to the soul of David. Pretty tight friendship! Linked together. What 'chained' them together was their humility as people; their innate sense of duty; their loyalty. But above all, they both possessed a heart for God.

Friendships are so important. Everyone needs friends; and everyone can be a friend to another. Fellowship implies a richness in that friendship, which brings such inner satisfaction. For in fellowship, one can share the greatest joys and the deepest sorrows. It's a strength for Christendom to have hearts 'chained' together in a godly bond of friendship.

Christ came to the world offering friendship and fellowship with us. In turn, he wants us to reach out to others, building relationships – friendships that are pure, wholesome, committed, and of God. It's divine communion.

Thought

Call a friend today and arrange to have fellowship together. Try also to make a *new* friend today, sharing God's love with them.

Returning Good for Evil

Saul asked, 'Is that your voice, David my son?' And he wept aloud (v. 16).

Saul knew he had lost favour with God. He knew he'd also lost a good friend and spiritual mentor in Samuel. He even knew his own son, Jonathan, had turned from him in allegiance with David – all because of Saul's changed behaviour.

Saul had certain remorse, as seen in today's Scripture; but he continued plotting against David. He was not just jealous and envious of this new leader on the rise; he was out to destroy him.

This same David had the perfect opportunity to kill the one who was so full of anger and hatred. It took place in the barren wilderness of En Gedi – in a cave. But because Saul was still God's anointed one, David simply cut off a piece of Saul's robe.

Later, he confronted Saul – showing he could have killed him, but didn't; asking him why he hated David so much. What had he done to get to this point of rage? Saul heard him out. He even referred to David as 'my son'. For he knew right from wrong; but it didn't last.

Sometimes people treat us badly. The natural tendency is to return evil for evil – revenge; retaliation. But the Lord wants us to turn it all over to him; to return *good* to the other, no matter what the circumstance. This takes humility. It takes Christlikeness.

It's interesting to note that the location of the once *wilderness* area of En Gedi is now a popular luxury resort community, halfway down the western coast of the Dead Sea. Something beautiful eventually emerging from something barren and deserted. Good for evil.

Thought

Today, look for a way to repay evil with something good – even letting go of a *not good* feeling about someone, and replacing it by paying that person a compliment. It does wonders for the soul!

Endings and Beginnings

And it came to pass after this, that David enquired of the LORD (v. 1, KJV).

Saul ended up taking his own life. After hearing that the Philistines had killed his sons, it was too much to bear. His life had amounted to nothing – having forfeited God for selfish ambitions. A *tragedy*. In modern English, this word is used to describe any adversity, no matter its cause. But more specifically, a tragedy is 'a calamity that results from a wrong decision based upon a flawed character'. Using this definition, Saul's life was a tragedy indeed.

David lamented for his close friend, Jonathan, who'd died in battle. But he also mourned for Saul, because he'd been God's anointed king. Saul – a man with such potential! Wasted . . .

'The beauty of Israel is slain upon thy high places: how are the mighty fallen!' (2 Samuel 1:19, KJV).

It was the end of an era. Saul's dynasty was short-lived because of the king's sin. But there was to be a new beginning, for David was soon anointed king over the house of Judah. There was certainly tension and turmoil at first with Ish-bosheth, Saul's surviving son, usurping the power in the north – resulting in civil war. But finally the opposition was removed, clearing the way for David at last to reign over a *united* kingdom.

Some things in life need to have a clear ending, certain closure. And although as human beings we don't have the capacity to forget certain things, we *do* have the ability – with God's grace – to move forward in his strength.

It's about forgiveness, for things people have done to us. It's about incentive, to move forward with a right attitude. It's about holiness, asking God's Spirit to dwell within.

Today is a new beginning, filled with great potential and wonderful possibilities. What will you do to bring ultimate joy to God's heart?

Bread

Then Jesus declared, 'I am the bread of life. He who comes to me will never go hungry, and he who believes in me will never be thirsty' (v. 35).

In this fourth Gospel, which is quite different from the first three 'synoptic' Gospels in its presentation, the whole aspect of faith or belief in Christ comes through strongly. In Chapter 6 we encounter two of the seven miracles of Jesus. The opening verses record the feeding of the 5,000 on the north shore of the Sea of Galilee. With the giving of a little bread from a child to Jesus, the miracle took place. People were fed. They then followed him to Capernaum the next day. They wanted another free meal.

You may have heard of the term 'rice Christians'. It's heard in some developing countries; people professing faith in Christ for the sake of food or services to be given. It's no different in the developed world. We could call them 'social Christians'. They join churches to make business contacts, for social networking.

Jesus knew why the people had followed him. They wanted more bread. The rich love it; the poor crave it. Yes, food is necessary for sustenance. But Jesus wanted the people to know there was so much more to life:

'Do not work for food that spoils, but for food that endures to eternal life, which the Son of Man will give you' (v. 27).

The people responded by asking what *works* they needed to do, what deeds were required, in order to be accepted by God. Jesus replied that the *work* of God is only one thing; to *believe* in Christ, to have faith in him, is of utmost importance. It's because Jesus *is* the Bread of Life. Belief and faith in Jesus is the only 'work' that makes us acceptable to God. The Bread of Life gives us all we will ever want, or need.

As we break bread with one another today, let's never forget the holy significance of bread.

Is Jesus the Christ?

Others said, 'He is the Christ' (v. 41).

It was the Feast of the Tabernacles, a time of thanksgiving. It commemorated the ending of the forty years of wandering in the wilderness, and people were gathering that autumn in Jerusalem to celebrate. Jesus' brothers encouraged him to travel from the safer area in Galilee south to Judea – to teach, preach and perform miracles there. His brothers went. Jesus also went, but in secret. Then, halfway through the feast he proceeded to the temple courts to teach. He told all who listened that his words came straight from God. Opinion was divided. Some thought he was a good man; others denounced him as a fraud.

When the children of Israel had wandered in the wilderness, food and water were scarce. But God had provided. So, in remembrance at their Feast of the Tabernacles, the priest each morning carried water from the Pool of Siloam in a golden pitcher – pouring it out as a drink offering at the time of the sacrifice. On the last and greatest day of the feast Jesus stood, saying:

'If anyone is thirsty, let him come to me and drink. Whoever believes in me . . . streams of living water will flow from within him' (vv. 37, 38).

After this declaration and invitation, the people were no doubt even more divided than before. Who is this man? Doesn't he come from Galilee? Could he be a prophet? Or is he a blatant deceiver?

People are no different today. They hear the message – then they're to respond. If they decide to believe in him, and are willing to drink of the living water, their thirst will be quenched – forever.

Prayer

Lord Jesus, you *are* the Christ – the living Son of God. Help me to share this life-giving, thirst-quenching news with someone who needs to hear it today.

Wisdom of the Ant

Go to the ant, you sluggard; consider its ways and be wise! (v. 6).

Ants can be extremely bothersome. Once they get into your house, it's hard to get rid of them. They invade picnic times, for they love to be social. We wish they'd simply all go away.

Do you know much about ants? There are over 8,800 known species – existing everywhere except in the North and South Pole regions. They turn most of the world's soil and actually enrich it. Ants eat ninety per cent of the corpses of small animals. They work hard; without them, hundreds of thousands of plant and animal species would become extinct and the world's ecosystem destabilised.

The ant is equipped with a sophisticated communication system. The purpose of life for an ant is its work, with its instinctive awareness to harvest for the winter and work for the good of the colony. The ant is all about diligence. The wisdom of the ant? Some might question or debate whether the ant is actually *wise*. Yet we can learn so much from this tiny 'bothersome' insect – and the poet-teacher of Proverbs knew it. There's so much work to be done for the kingdom of God. Yet if we become lazy, sluggish, willing to leave God's work for others, much will be lost. *People* will be lost. And this just can't happen.

Jesus himself said he was to do the 'work' of God who sent him. It was a sacred task. *Ours* is a sacred task. Antonio Stradivari, the world's greatest violin maker, once said, 'If my hand slacked, I should rob God.' He knew who he was created to be, and what to do, for his God. Christ wants us to use our skills wisely, as we work for him.

The wisdom of the ant; the wisdom of God's people. May we always be diligent in everything we do, according to the Spirit's leading.

Prayer

Lord, as your faithful stewards, help us to be wise in the building of your kingdom here on earth.

Weaver Divine

What you heard from me, keep as the pattern of sound teaching, with faith and love in Christ Jesus (v. 13).

I greatly admire those who are quilters; those who patiently, and creatively, work on quilts that end up being gorgeous masterpieces. Many of us have been the beneficiaries of a hand-made quilt. They are warm and cosy, as well as being so very *personal*. Just before the 'backing' of the quilt is put on, it's fascinating to observe the 'mess', the disastrous disorder on the *reverse* side. Threads criss-crossing everywhere, in what looks like total confusion.

So true when we go our own way. Things get totally messed up. Life begins to rapidly unravel, and we don't know how to make things right again. How we need Christ to weave us into something beautiful; to make a 'pattern' of our life that is beyond our imagination:

> Weaver divine, thy matchless skill
> Hath planned the pattern of my ways;
> Within the fabric of thy will
> I yield my residue of days.
>
> *(SASB 644)*

People often think the Christian life is predictable, colourless, restricted. I want my life to be filled with colour; to *reflect* a pattern that is like no other – all because of the Divine Weaver:

> Christ of the loom, thy loving hand
> Doth thread the pattern for my good;
> I too would weave at thy command
> Until thy will be understood. (v. 4)

The author of these words, Brindley Boon, suggests here that we, too, can take part in the weaving as we reach out to others. Yes, Weaver Divine, create in me your heart's desire – so I can be your instrument in taking your love to others.

David's Prayer

'How great you are, O Sovereign LORD! There is no-one like you, and there is no God but you' (v. 22).

David didn't have an easy road to the throne. But he was honest before God. He trusted God for the ultimate outcome, knowing deep within that all would be according to God's plan. All he wanted was to be used for God's glory. And because of this, God made David a promise, delivered by his servant, Nathan:

'I will raise up your offspring . . . Your house and your kingdom shall endure for ever' (vv. 12, 16).

No doubt David couldn't comprehend what this meant; that God would send his only Son, through David's line, to save and redeem the whole world. He could never grasp the implications of God's promise to him on that day, a promise that would change the world forever. But he definitely felt the impact of that holy moment in time, as he *sat* before the Lord, in all humility, and said:

'Who am I, O Sovereign LORD?' (v. 18).

This is why God chose David. He wasn't perfect. Everyone who reads of his life is fully aware of this. But his family 'line' was to be blessed; the 'house' of David would always be remembered. For through him would come the Messiah.

Today is the birthday of my eldest son, Joel. When he was in the womb, I was advised to abort because of complications. I didn't, praying that this unborn child would be a true blessing. Joel was born, perfectly healthy. He has grown up to love God and is a wonderful blessing today to me, to his wife, to others. My house, blessed – through faith, trust, in the Almighty.

Prayer

Today, pray not just David's prayer but *your* prayer. Pray that your house – for now and always – will be truly blessed by God.

Mephibosheth

Mephibosheth lived in Jerusalem, because he always ate at the king's table, and he was crippled in both feet (v. 13).

David had every right to harbour hatred toward Saul's family. Yet one day he asked Ziba, who had been a servant of King Saul, if there was anyone still alive from the house of Saul. He told King David that there was Jonathan's son – who was crippled in both feet. David immediately sent for him.

Mephibosheth arrived, terrified for what might take place. He felt his life was definitely on the line. Surely David would want him dead, so all Saul's descendants would be gone forever. But a strange turn of events took place instead. Not only did David spare his life; he restored to him all the land that belonged to Saul. And in addition Mephibosheth would, from then on, eat at the king's table. Ziba, along with his family members and servants, would be responsible for farming this newly restored land for Saul's grandson.

Kindness. It's a beautiful quality in a person. There's something quite lovely about a real act of kindness shown toward another. It touches the heart. Here he was, king of such a large and powerful territory, no doubt so many things on his mind: military strategy, managing the kingdom, getting ready to go to battle himself. Yet David paused . . . wanting to honour the former king, who had hated him so much. He put aside any power issues, any thoughts of revenge, to inquire about a relative of Saul's that he could help in some way. He wanted to shower him with God's kindness.

It's a very tender story, showing something wonderful about David's character. It reveals something of his *heart*.

Today, think of at least one random act of kindness you can show toward someone who would really benefit from it. May it be God's loving kindness shining through you.

You are the Man!

'Now, therefore, the sword will never depart from your house, because you despised me and took the wife of Uriah the Hittite to be your own' (v. 10).

David won victory after victory. Things were going extremely well for him. He was both powerful and popular. But he was also human. On the outside, he was doing well. But on the inside, things were going to his head. His eyes were not focused on the Lord. He soon *saw*; he *desired*; he then *took*. The repercussions – devastating.

When Nathan, instructed by God, presented a certain scenario to David concerning a little ewe lamb, David lashed out in rage:

'The man who did this deserves to die!' (v. 5).

Nathan quickly responded to the king:

'You are the man!' (v. 7).

The consequences for David? There would be continual turmoil and devastation in the king's family. Also, the child conceived with Bathsheba would die. But above all, David knew he had sinned against God: adultery with Bathsheba, then the murder of Uriah.

We quickly point the finger at David: How could he be a true man of God? What an ungodly person he really was! He didn't deserve to be king at all. He shouldn't be a descendant of the Messiah. But we must look at ourselves. What do we *deserve*? Let's think of some of the things we've done in the past. Are we proud of them? Do we deserve to be God's precious child? The power of sin is huge. But, the power of forgiveness is beyond our comprehension.

David needed to confront *himself*, taking full responsibility for his sin against God. He needed God to create a *clean* heart; to renew a *right* spirit within. If we're harbouring sin, we need to confess it. We then must ask the Holy Spirit to cleanse *all* that's within – so we can be white as snow!

Prayer

Lord, this is *my* prayer today: 'Create in me a clean heart, O God, and renew a right, persevering, and steadfast spirit within me' (Psalm 51:10, *AB*).

Concert of Prayer

'Do not leave Jerusalem, but wait for the gift my Father promised, which you have heard me speak about' (v. 4).

In the book of Acts, Luke records for us how the early Church came to be established. It speaks to the hardships, the persecutions. But it mostly speaks to how this little band of followers took all they knew – then shared it with others, turning the world upside down.

Just before the ascension, Jesus candidly spoke to his apostles. He told them they were to wait for the promised gift – before going out into the world to proclaim his name. They needed the Holy Spirit to come upon them if they were to take on the enormous task of establishing his kingdom on earth, if they were to spread the good news to Jerusalem, Judea and Samaria, and to the ends of the earth.

It was to be the beginning of something new and exciting. It was the establishment of a new way of thinking and believing. The long-awaited Messiah had come, lived among his people; and because he would no longer be with them physically, his Holy Spirit would come upon them – in order that they carry on Christ's mission. He would indwell *all* those who believed in Jesus.

They couldn't do anything in their own strength. This is why Jesus told them to wait. They returned from the Mount of Olives to an upper room. Others joined them: Mary, Jesus' mother, his brothers. It became a concert of prayer – offered, as they waited for the gift.

It's a sacred time, waiting upon the Lord. What does he want us to do? Where does he want us to go? What is the Holy Spirit saying to me, today? A *concert* of prayer is a beautiful concept, for there's no set structure – only a 'concert' of heart-cries, given to the King of kings. Present this offering, this concert of prayer, to your Lord today. You will be blessed, as you wait upon him.

His Provision

All of them were filled with the Holy Spirit (v. 4).

The great English preacher, Charles Spurgeon, once said: 'We might preach 'til our tongue rotted, 'til we exhaust our lungs and die – but never a soul would be converted unless the Holy Spirit uses the Word to convert that soul'.[6] Following the ascension, and after the apostles waited upon the Lord, the Holy Spirit came upon them like a mighty wind. They were ready to take on the task Jesus had for them, for they were now empowered – filled with the Spirit.

They could easily have 'passed' on the *waiting* period. They could have felt rather self-confident, having walked with the Master for three years. They could have felt qualified with their apostolic credentials. But nothing would have happened that would have lasted. Nothing would have taken place that would have impacted the people, and hence the world at large. At Pentecost, the Holy Spirit came, igniting them. This gave them courage to speak forth in Jesus' name, despite all the opposition they faced. Nothing could have happened without the provision of God's Holy Spirit.

Sometimes we think we can do things in our own strength. We get all the education, and feel this is enough. We get all the experience of years working in ministry, and think this is enough. All these things are important, are valuable; but without the infilling of the Holy Spirit, all is in vain.

It begins with you, and with me. It begins with a people of prayer – humble, holy people. It begins with the full awareness of our need for a fresh anointing of God's Spirit upon our lives. As one Army, one Church, may we echo the chorus of a song written by Retired General John Gowans:

> Holy Spirit, Promised Presence fall on me.
> Holy Spirit, make me all I long to be.
> Holy Spirit, Holy Spirit,
> Give your power to me, O Holy Spirit![7]

Belonging

I love you, O LORD, my strength (v. 1).

There's nothing quite like loving someone, and being loved in return. The psalmist says it all in the opening verse – sharing and expressing his love for God. You sense he is saying this *in response* to God's expression of love toward him. In fact, he makes reference to these love-expressions from God throughout the psalm itself.

God has been David's *rock*, his *deliverer* – saving him from his enemies. God has been his *salvation*, his *stronghold*. God heard David's cry for help. He then reached down and *rescued* David. Why? Because David 'belonged' to him; he *delighted* in David.

In our fractured world, many feel detached; so alone, even isolated. Young men join gangs, just to belong. Young women can get into unhealthy relationships, just to feel they belong to someone. However, true and healthy belonging has to begin with our relationship with the Creator. He longs for us to have a strong, beautiful, intimate relationship with him. Then he waits for our response. And he'll go to the extreme to make sure we know we're loved and belong to him.

Later in the psalm it says:

You stoop down to make me great (v. 35).

Just consider the imagery presented here: God 'stooping down' to build us up. God, bending over, reaching down, stretching out – for you, and for me. How beautiful! God, looking down at me, who is stumbling and messing things up; yet still having that desire and longing to 'stoop' and pick me up. He doesn't do it out of pity; but to actually make me *great*. Why? Because I *belong* to him!

Prayer

Father, many days I fail you; yet you stoop down to raise me again. Thank you for loving me; for allowing me to belong to you.

Sweet Hour of Prayer

Do not be anxious about anything, but in everything, by prayer and petition, with thanksgiving, present your requests to God (v. 6).

We live in an extremely busy world. We bustle from one activity to another. Everyone's in a hurry. And it seems that, if we're not extremely rushed, something is desperately wrong.

> Sweet hour of prayer, sweet hour of prayer,
> That calls me from a world of care.
> (William Walford, *SASB* 633)

An *hour* of prayer? How can we afford this amount of time when there's so much to be done, and our minds are constantly racing? Maybe some day there'll be more time. But for now, people seem to be preoccupied with so many distractions and various activities going on.

Yet, a day has twenty-four hours. Is it unreasonable to think that *one* of these hours be devoted to the One we love so dearly? If not an hour, at least *half* an hour? Does our Lord not deserve at least this? Is it something we actually need to *pray* about? He wants, so very much, for us to be in direct contact *with* him:

> And since he bids me seek his face,
> Believe his word and trust his grace,
> I'll cast on him my every care
> And wait for thee, sweet hour of prayer. (v. 2)

He wants us to be excited about our time with him. To greatly anticipate waiting upon the Lord – in prayer! The benefits? The *fruit* that will come of it? Sweet, intimate communion with God the Father!

> Put off this robe of flesh, and rise
> To gain the everlasting prize,
> And realise for ever there
> The fruits of the sweet hour of prayer. (v. 3)

Family Trials

The king covered his face and cried aloud, 'O my son Absalom! O Absalom, my son, my son!' (v. 4).

When David took his eyes away from the Lord, sinning against him, he was suddenly filled with a sense of deep remorse. Yes, he was forgiven; but he had to pay the consequences. His *house* would be in turmoil.

And it was! We soon learn of what went on between Amnon and Tamar, two of his children by different mothers. Amnon had very strong desires for his half-sister, Tamar. He faked being sick, so she would come in to care for him. He grabbed her and forced himself upon her. He then threw her away as trash. She was damaged, for life.

Tamar's brother, Absalom, soon heard of what went on. Defending the honour of his sister, he had his half-brother killed. Soon after this, Absalom's ambition got the better of him – seeking the throne for himself. He mocked the king by sleeping with David's concubines, out in the open.

King David was forced to protect the throne, and the kingdom, against his own son. When heading to battle, he said to his men:

'Be gentle with the young man Absalom for my sake' (18:5).

The victory was David's; but his son was killed in the battle. The king *grieved* for his son, who had turned on him. Deep family trials; deep personal sorrow, gripping at David's heart.

When we contemplate going against God, sinning, we don't think ahead to the consequences – the ripple effect, the way others in our family will react, the way things will play out in life. The repercussions can affect us profoundly. And so, today, let's pray for purity of thought and holiness of heart. May *all* we do be for God's glory alone.

Heart for God

'The Spirit of the LORD spoke through me; his word was on my tongue'
(v. 2).

Some might rightly ask why David, with all the sins he committed, was still so mightily used of God. It is indeed a mystery. Yet only God sees what's deep inside a person. From what we read in Scripture, we know for certain David had a heart for God. He wasn't perfect. Far from it! He made some terrible mistakes. Yet he was, through it all, made fully aware of God's mercy, his forgiveness. He loved God supremely.

Because he was still a man of war, he wasn't allowed to build the temple for God – something he desperately wanted to do. This privilege was to be for his son Solomon, his name derived from the word meaning peace – *shalom*. David was to spend his last days preparing Solomon for what lay ahead. Having a heart for God meant he had a heart for God's glory, his work, and God's people.

Glory. The tabernacle had been the centre of worship in the past. In it was the ark of the covenant, symbolising God's presence. But the Israelites were no longer a nomadic people. They needed a place of worship, where they could glorify God.

Work. The Israelites were not just to build a structure. Their work was to be seen as glorifying God. They were to have a heart for working, for serving God. They were to work with joy and thanksgiving for all God had done for them.

People. David had a heart for God's people. He wanted his family, friends, the subjects of his kingdom to know God and to serve him. Battles could be won; kingdoms could be theirs. But if the people did not serve God, it was all in vain.

David had a heart for God, serving him until the end. Today is a new day, with all the tomorrows ahead. Let's have a heart only for God – giving him all glory in our work and service for him.

Going Home

*The LORD moved the heart of Cyrus king of Persia to make a
proclamation throughout his realm and to put it in writing (v. 1).*

The year is 538 BC. The Jews have been held captive for seventy years and
are finally allowed to return to their homeland. The beginning of the
book of Ezra speaks of a decree, issued by the king of Persia, permitting this
to take place.

The first group is getting ready to return under the leadership of
Zerubbabel. Their goal? Upon returning, they would rebuild the temple –
prophesied by Isaiah 200 years earlier:

*'I am the LORD . . . who says of Cyrus, "He is my shepherd and will
accomplish all that I please; he will say of Jerusalem, 'Let it be rebuilt,' and of
the temple, 'Let its foundations be laid'"' (Isaiah 44:24, 28).*

It's interesting to note here that the pagan king, Cyrus, is used as the Lord's
instrument. And so, the people pack up their lives and get ready for the long
900-mile journey ahead of them. A detailed list is given of those who returned
– more than 50,000 priests, carpenters, masons; then all the common folk,
with all their families. The thought of going *home*, at last, spurs them on.

They finally arrive, needing to find both food and shelter; but the very first
thing they feel compelled to do is to worship God. They instinctively knew
that the ultimate success of all their ventures depended upon the attitude of
their hearts toward him:

*On the first day of the seventh month they began to offer burnt offerings to
the LORD, though the foundations of the LORD's temple had not yet been laid
(Ezra 3:6).*

Many things always seem to pile up; tasks to be done, to be completed. But
first things first. Before attempting anything, we must worship God, with
thankfulness of heart.

I Have a Dream

'In the last days, God says, I will pour out my Spirit on all people. Your sons and daughters will prophesy, your young men will see visions, your old men will dream dreams' (v. 17).

The civil rights leader in the USA, Dr Martin Luther King Jr, saw the devastation taking place all around in his country. In August 1963, he spoke to his nation – to the world – of his dream: 'I have a dream that my four little children will one day live in a nation where they will not be judged by the colour of their skin but by the content of their character. I have a dream today!'

It was a dream of equality, of opportunity; a dream where all would live in harmony and peace. It was not just one man's desire. It was a national, an international, dream; a hope for the future – to respect all, living with an integrity of heart.

It was God's 'dream' that the good news of Jesus be spread to all the world. It was to begin right in Jerusalem. Peter, empowered by the Holy Spirit, addressed the crowd who had witnessed the baptism of the Holy Spirit upon Jesus' followers. He was quick to remind them of the prophetic words of Joel, that there would be prophecies, visions, dreams, wonders, signs. This would happen when God poured out his Spirit upon his people.

What were they to make of this? If the people accepted Christ, becoming Spirit-filled, what would happen to them? What will happen to people today? Several things will take place. First, we'll be filled with *joy*; the infectious joy of the Lord. Second, we'll become *unified*. Spirit-filled people are of one spirit. And third, we'll become *ambassadors* for Christ – reaching out, telling others of his wondrous power.

Martin Luther King had a dream. God has an even greater dream for us; to share his Son, Jesus Christ, with all who will hear. It's a dream that can become a transformational reality!

Exuberance

They followed a daily discipline of worship in the Temple followed by meals at home, every meal a celebration, exuberant and joyful, as they praised God. People in general liked what they saw. Every day their number grew as God added those who were saved (vv. 46, 47, MSG).

Those early Christians loved to eat! Oh yes, they went to worship, and no doubt had sincerity of heart. But they also enjoyed simply being together and eating together; they enjoyed Christian fellowship – for they were celebrating, as brothers and sisters in Christ. And when others saw it, saw their joy and exuberance and genuine happiness, they wanted to be part of it all.

Have you ever been part of a church service that is joy*less*, having a real lack of exuberance? I have. It's not a good nor an uplifting experience. We need joy! Maybe we need to have more food, or more music, to draw others into this enriching fellowship – for it's a bond like no other. Why? Because Christ is at the centre of it all.

The great English poet William Blake said, 'Exuberance is beauty.' The French writer Gustave Flaubert went further to say, 'Exuberance is better than taste.' To be *exuberant* over something is to be so excited, so involved, so convinced that something is good and wonderful, that you give your all. Worshipping God is a wonderful, exuberant experience!

Scripture tells us they *devoted* themselves to the apostles' teaching, to prayer. They shared what they had with one another – even to the point of selling possessions. They praised God, in all of this, with great *exuberance*. Not a fluffy kind of faith; not just an emotional outburst here and there. It was genuine, coming from within; contagious, exciting. People, because of it, were saved.

May we all have a renewed *exuberance* as we worship God today, and the days to follow. May our faces shine, radiate, glow, in order that people see Christ in us. And because of our exuberance and joy, may people continue to be saved.

The Heavens Declare

The heavens declare the glory of God; the skies proclaim the work of his hands (v. 1).

What a marvellous psalm this is! It is undoubtedly one of my favourites, and perhaps yours as well; for when reading it, we can become transfixed in awe before God's magnificent creation. It's a creation that, in itself, is 'declaring' who God is – in order that all people may behold his glory and majesty.

Sir Christopher Wren built the magnificent St Paul's Cathedral in London, England, and is buried there. On his tombstone it says, translated from the Latin, 'If you wish to see his monument, look around you.' Beauty. Majesty. Spendour.

And so, we can gaze into the vast sky at night, splashed with the brilliance of a million stars; or we can feel the sun in the day, giving warmth to animals, life to trees and flowers. Creation declares God's glory; and we are witnesses to the signature of God on all his handiwork.

But our faith in him goes further than even the beauty of his creation. The psalmist reveals to us God's truth of who he is, and what he means to us in a very personal and intimate way. What, then, is our response? What do we say to a God who loves us in such a profound way? The psalmist, wanting to give fully of himself to his God, responds this way:

May the words of my mouth and the meditation of my heart be pleasing in your sight, O LORD, my Rock and my Redeemer (v. 14).

All I say, all I think – wanting to be *pleasing* before the Lord. My life, to be a sweet fragrance, offered wholly to him; an aroma that is sweet to God, bringing honour and glory to his name. This is *my* declaration, *my* heart's desire. Will it be yours today?

Love Divine

See how I love your precepts; preserve my life, O LORD, according to your love (v. 159).

So often we sing hymns without giving full attention to the profound lyrics. This hymn of Charles Wesley is rich in theology, as it speaks to the incarnation, gives reference to the crucifixion and resurrection, then emphasises the indwelling Spirit for all believers:

> Love divine, all loves excelling, Joy of Heaven, to earth come down,
> Fix in us thy humble dwelling, All thy faithful mercies crown.
> Jesus, thou art all compassion, Pure, unbounded love thou art;
> Visit us with thy salvation, Enter every longing heart.
>
> (SASB 438)

When we sing such a powerful hymn, it evokes from us a response. We sing these words, and should immediately want to lift our hearts to God in adoration and praise; to say or do something, in order to show our deep love and gratitude – just for who he is.

I've been a Rotarian for more than fifteen years. I greatly enjoy being part of this unique international fellowship. This service club is humanitarian in its desire to reach out both to people in the community and also internationally. Rotary's motto is 'Service Above Self', which is admirable and indeed noble.

Yet Christian faith goes even deeper. Yes, we want to meet the physical needs of others; but far more than this, we want to share God's divine love with all who will hear; telling of his grace, mercy, love, compassion. It begins with us being a holy people – then pointing them to a Love that will change them, forever.

> Finish then thy new creation, Pure and spotless let us be;
> Let us see thy great salvation, Perfectly restored in thee.
> Changed from glory into glory, Till in Heaven we take our place,
> Till we cast our crowns before thee, Lost in wonder, love and praise. (v. 3)

Convictions

'We alone will build it for the LORD, the God of Israel, as King Cyrus, the king of Persia, commanded us' (v. 3).

The people began to rebuild the temple; to restore their identity as a people. But there was an issue. Zerubbabel refused to let the enemies of Judah and Benjamin assist in the building. He felt convicted that this was an assignment for God's people alone. What followed was legal action – halting the work for fifteen years.

Finally, with the prophets Haggai and Zechariah speaking encouragement into the situation, a declaration came from King Darius. The construction began again, and the temple was soon built – a cause for great national celebration.

Most of us have convictions about certain things. They might have to do with our faith, or family. Convictions are good and right, if they align with God's will for our life. Zerubbabel no doubt wanted the temple built as soon as possible, just like everyone else. But his strong conviction was that it should be done with no pagan interference. There was great opposition; but he held firm, knowing it was God's will. God's work was to be done in God's way. Perseverance is often the difference between failure and success.

The temple was built. Both Haggai and Zechariah gave the people a new vision of God's work. The glory of this house would exceed the glory of the former edifice – knowing that the Messiah would one day come to the temple:

'Be strong, O Zerubbabel . . . For I am with you . . . The glory of this present house will be greater than the glory of the former house . . . in this place I will grant peace' (Haggai 2:4, 9).

Because of a strong conviction, glory came – and there was peace. Let's be strong in our convictions, asking always for the Lord's guidance and direction.

Direction

Ezra had devoted himself to the study and observance of the Law of the LORD, and to teaching its decrees and laws in Israel (v. 10).

Fifty-eight years pass, after the completion of the temple. Ezra, a priest still in Babylon, is now ready to guide a second company of Jews back to Jerusalem, to oversee the affairs of the temple and to provide the nation with leadership. The king allows them to leave, providing for them the necessities for worship.

Ezra was one of the great Scripture scholars of his day. But he was more than a teacher; his heart burned for God's Word, the law of the Lord. It wasn't simply head knowledge; it was heart knowledge. His goal was to give spiritual *direction* for his people; to rebuild the people spiritually. He didn't need manpower; he needed ministers – people willing to be there for others.

Our prayer life is so critical; for it's all about the effect of our prayers upon others, or other situations, that can never be taken for granted. God's Word must penetrate our hearts, then be translated into a life that reaches out to others, as God would have us be used. It's all about following his direction for our life.

Many of us have travelled by plane, yet most of us would be oblivious to how a pilot gets from point A to point B. Most likely, the pilot uses VOR, short for VHF Omni-Directional Radio Range, a navigational system invented in the early 1950s. The pilot sets the course of the aircraft on his dial. If the aircraft drifts from that set course, the instrument shows the pilot that the plane is deviating – so he can correct it to align the aircraft to the set course again.

Just as Ezra used God's Word as his navigational system, we are to do likewise; guided in the direction that is pleasing to God.

Prayer

Lord, help me to continue loving your Word. Affirm in me the direction you would have me go – so I can be your instrument. Help me also to guide others in their daily faith journey.

Reformation

'Now make confession to the LORD, the God of your fathers, and do his will. Separate yourselves . . .' (v. 11).

The temple was built; leadership was in place. But there needed to be purity within. All marriage relationships with foreign women were to be annulled, for pagan influence would draw people away from God. Ezra is broken with sadness over this, for he knew it would cause the breaking-up of families. Yet, painful as it was, he knew it was necessary. The people could not be unequally yoked, for there would be divided spiritual hearts. Reformation was essential.

Reformation of any kind isn't easy. The great Protestant Reformation, which began with Martin Luther in Germany – when he nailed his ninety-five theses to the wooden door of the Castle Church in Wittenberg on 31 October 1517 – was not easy at all. Many ended up losing their lives because of their convictions and desire for reform. Yet reformation was necessary, for *all* concerned.

Ezra told the people that they must first confess; then, they were to *separate* themselves from all that was not of God – which included their non-Jewish wives. A complete reformation was needed, if they were to be a holy people. They listened, and they were willing to be obedient; for they knew they were God's chosen people. They knew they had sinned, and wanted to come clean before God.

Some things can creep into our church, into our lives, that are not of God. We can become so used to these things that they don't even seem wrong any longer. The Lord asks that we look deep, to see if there's anything hindering our spiritual walk with him: a habit, a relationship, a sin. Then, we're to confess it – and give it up, completely. Only then can we be a holy people.

May his restorative love, and grace, be ours this day.

For Jesus' Sake

*'Lord, do not hold this sin against them.' When he said this, he fell asleep.
And Saul was there, giving approval to his death (vv. 60, 1).*

The apostles were empowered by the Holy Spirit to preach the good news
of Christ. They had courage and authority, seeing wonderful results.
Even when Peter and John were first thrown into prison, Scripture records
that five thousand came to faith – and this was probably just the men who
were counted.

The apostles had to endure much persecution and suffering for their faith.
But they were more than willing, because they were doing it for Jesus' sake.
This is what witnessing meant. The persecution from without and pressure
from within only helped to unite the believers in a strong bond of fellowship
and purpose. In fact, it enlarged the outreach in their community.

The early Church was expanding so quickly that they needed others to
help with leadership. Seven were chosen. Certain qualifications were required
– the most important being that they were to be filled with the Spirit. But soon
one of the seven, Stephen, was seized. False charges of blasphemy were laid on
him – for seemingly going against all that was Jewish.

Stephen could have recanted. But he defended himself by saying his faith
was in Moses, but above all in God and his Son, Jesus Christ. It's recorded
that his face was 'like . . . an angel' (Acts 6:15). He radiated Christ's beauty.

Knowing he was going to be stoned, Stephen lifted his eyes to heaven and
saw Jesus 'standing' at God's right hand – the only account in Scripture of
Jesus *standing* in heaven – no doubt ready to receive his servant.

People today still face persecution because of their faith. They do it, all for
Jesus' sake. We pray for them; for courage, faithfulness. I believe Jesus stands
for *them* – ready to receive them into his loving arms.

Prayer

**Father, help me always to think beyond myself and my immediate
circumstances. Be with others who are in great need of you today.**

To Be Like Jesus

'Who are you, Lord?' Saul asked. 'I am Jesus, whom you are persecuting,'
he replied. 'Now get up and go into the city, and you will be told what
you must do' (vv. 5, 6).

It was revolutionary thinking for the Jewish people – to believe Jesus was the
promised Messiah. Then, after he ascended to heaven, to have faith to
believe Jesus *was* truly the Son of God. But many believed it all to be true.
And they wanted to emulate him, in every way possible. To be like him.

It's transformational thinking for us today, to leave behind a secular
lifestyle in order to be like Jesus. For it's a new way of thinking; a life of
humility, sacrifice, service, giving. But then, a life of *holiness*? Being Spirit-
filled? For some, it's just far too much.

It's about faith, conversion, deep spirituality, a relationship. The Salvation
Army has published a number of musicals. *Spirit* is one of these, based on the
early Church. A simple chorus comes from it:

> To be like Jesus! This hope possesses me,
> In every thought and deed, this is my aim, my creed;
> To be like Jesus! This hope possesses me,
> His Spirit helping me, like him I'll be.
>
> (*SASB* chorus 107)

To be like Jesus! It's possible only by his Spirit.

Saul, persecutor of the early Christians, had an encounter with Jesus on the
road to Damascus. It was like no other, for God knew Saul was to be the one
who would spread the good news of Jesus to so many – including the
Gentiles. Before he could be used of God, Saul needed to be filled with the
Holy Spirit. After being blinded, he eventually received his 'sight' – both
physically and spiritually. He then, as Paul, wanted to be like Jesus. The same
is possible for us all!

Victory!

We will shout for joy when you are victorious and will lift up our banners in the name of our God (20:5).

Psalm 20 is a song, written before going to war. It was to be sung to the king by a choir or congregation – to give inspiration; a prayer that God would be with the warriors in the battle, and that victory would be theirs. Even though there's potential danger ahead, the psalm breathes an atmosphere of confidence and trust in God.

We can all relate to this kind of psalm, for we all face battles. And when they come, and we turn to God in prayer, the psalmist says to us concerning the outcome:

May he give you the desire of your heart (v. 4).

Fighting battles alone is difficult. We're defeated before we even start. Having someone with us makes all the difference. Knowing for certain God is also with us makes the battle far less frightening. For the Lord always goes before us. Then, it's having the faith to believe he will intervene with the saving power of his right hand (v. 6). He only wants the very best for us, no matter what we're facing. He only wants there to be victory.

Psalm 21 follows, this time immediately expressing thanksgiving for the battle won. In response to verse 4 above, it says of God:

You have granted him the desire of his heart (v. 2).

Victory! The battle won, the foe conquered! The psalmist glories in the abundance of God's help through the difficult times – when the battles and trials come. Here, God places a 'crown of pure gold' on David's head, because of his trust in God. As he blesses David, so does he desire to bless us – so that victory will be ours.

Yes, battles come; but they can be overcome, when our faith is in the Lord. May today be a day of victory!

My Life – Broken Bread

While they were eating, Jesus took bread, gave thanks and broke it, and gave it to his disciples, saying, 'Take it; this is my body' (v. 22).

The following, written by General Albert Orsborn, is The Salvation Army's sacramental offering to the Lord:

> My life must be Christ's broken bread, My love his outpoured wine,
> A cup o'erfilled, a table spread Beneath his name and sign,
> That other souls, refreshed and fed, May share his life through mine.
> *(SASB 512)*

Although Salvationists do not use the *elements* in our services, we *are* a sacramental Army, a sacramental movement within the body of Christ. All our work is sacramental, for it is unto Jesus. Verse 2 tells us that we are to give all we have to him, to be used by him:

> My all is in the Master's hands, For him to bless and break.

Sometimes people question The Salvation Army because of its stand on the sacraments. I recall once, when taking my Masters of Theological Studies degree, a professor criticising the Army for its viewpoint. I was glad to have this song to share with him; for we *are* sacramental. Christ in us.

May we live according to the grace we receive. May we continue to be blessed, broken, by the Master. For one day, we will rise and live with him – for eternity!

> Lord, let me share that grace of thine Wherewith thou didst sustain
> The burden of the fruitful vine, The gift of buried grain.
> Who dies with thee, O Word divine, Shall rise and live again. (v. 3)

Divine Permission

In all this, Job did not sin by charging God with wrongdoing (v. 22).

The book of Job examines one of life's most perplexing questions – suffering. In a sudden series of catastrophes, Job loses his family, fame, fortune and fitness. There are extensive, soul-searching debates with his best friends – desperately trying to find a reason for his misfortunes. Finally, Job is confronted by God himself.

We begin in the land of Uz, south-east of the Dead Sea. This area in North Arabia was a ranching region, containing lots of cattle and sheep. It was the home of the wealthy herdsman Job, a man who led an exemplary life for God. In the heavenly realm, unknown to Job but known to the reader, a drama takes place. Satan accuses Job of serving God, only for material reward. God gives permission for Satan to test Job, by taking away everything important to him.

Most of us aren't wealthy. Yet what if everything was taken – and we were left with absolutely nothing; no home, no food, no clothing? It would be difficult; we'd wonder *why*.

Most of us aren't famous; but we do have a reputation. What if our reputation was smeared, our character attacked – when we'd done nothing wrong? Or what if we became very sick, living with disabling physical ailments? It would be extremely hard, and we'd wonder *why*. Family is important to us. What if suddenly all were taken, all gone from Earth forever? Devastating! Surely, we'd wonder *why*. We even might ask why God would give permission for Job, or anyone, to be tested in this way.

This book is not just about pain and suffering. It's about faith, life, love. For after Job loses *everything* that matters to him, we see that the one thing that could *not* be taken was his relationship with God. At the end of all Job's tragedy, it says:

Then he fell to the ground in worship (v. 20).

Three Friends

No-one said a word to him, because they saw how great his suffering was (2:13).

Everyone needs friends. Here we're introduced to Job's three friends: Eliphaz, Bildad and Zophar. They heard what had happened to their good friend, Job. For seven days and nights they did the very best thing possible; they simply sat with Job, and said nothing. Their presence was enough. It showed they loved and deeply cared for their friend.

But their wisdom soon turned into selfish outbursts, for they relied on their own wisdom rather than God's. Their human, self-centred personalities took over as they began to tell Job what they each thought was the root cause of Job's profound suffering. During the course of this first debate, the main issue they raise is that all suffering results from sin. In other words, Job must have done something terrible to cause all the tragedy he was experiencing. For not only did he lose everything important and precious to him, not only was he suffering physically, but he was also suffering from a severe depression – which was affecting everything he was doing in life. The three friends told him to confess the sin and get on with it. But Job had *not* sinned. He had been faithful to his God.

Despite all that had been said, despite all the suffering he was enduring, Job knew it was not because of sin in his life. He still had his integrity. He didn't have the answer to the *whys*; but he knew his God was sovereign, in control of all things – including his own life. His faith, his hope in God for the future, was ever present:

'Though he slay me, yet will I hope in him' (13:15).

Job knew justice would prevail, and he'd one day be *vindicated*. It was, and is, all about complete trust in God.

Broken Heart

'My friends scorn me; my eye pours out tears to God' (v. 20, NRSV).

The verbal attacks continue as the three 'counsellors' move into their second cycle of debates. They describe Job's world as worthless, denying that he understands anything of God. They say he's naïve, perhaps even simple-minded, a narrow thinker.

Although Job rejects all the bitter accusations, within himself he agonises over God's apparent plot to destroy him. Depression begins to creep in, for there seems to be no light. Hope seems to be snuffed out. His heart is broken.

There are many broken hearts out there. People who have been deeply wounded; people who are presently suffering from emotional or physical pain; people who have been rejected by those they love and trusted. Many survive from a broken body; but it's extremely difficult to be healed from a broken heart. Job sensed that he was doomed, defeated:

'All was well with me, but he shattered me; he seized me by the neck and crushed me' (v. 12).

Difficult words to say. And it wasn't just about him; he claimed that God had devastated his entire household. All were 'broken'. Job admits that his face was 'red with weeping' (v. 16). Yet through his brokenness, through his depression, he could still pray – knowing he had an advocate in heaven, speaking on his behalf:

'He that vouches for me is on high' (v. 19, NRSV).

Some might be angry with God. Others, simply baffled by the fact that God would allow such pain, agony, suffering to enter their lives. Whether or not we're presently suffering from a broken heart, we no doubt know of at least one person who is. Be a friend to them; also, let God know that you trust him – implicitly.

A Vision

While Peter was still speaking these words, the Holy Spirit came on all who heard the message (v. 44).

Caesarea was a Roman colony, the capital of Judea. Many Greeks lived in Caesarea, including Cornelius. He was a centurion, the captain of a 'century' or band, consisting of anywhere from one to six hundred soldiers. He was a Gentile worshipper, a 'proselyte of the gate'. While praying at the ninth hour, about three o'clock, an angel appeared, telling him to send men to Joppa – now Jaffa – to seek out a man called Peter, at the house of Simon the Tanner.

The next day at the sixth hour, toward noon, Peter was praying on a rooftop and fell into a trance – the only *trance* recorded in Scripture. He had an unusual vision of a sheet, the four corners representing the four corners of the earth. On this sheet were all kinds of animals – clean and unclean. Three times a *voice* told him to eat. When Peter said he couldn't eat anything unclean, the voice told him that *everything* God made was pure (vv. 9–16).

Peter came out of the trance and just sat, *wondering about the meaning of the vision* (v. 17). Then the Spirit told him three men would come to the house. He was to go with them.

The sequence is important, seeing the beautiful working of the Spirit. He spoke to Cornelius, preparing him through the angel. The next day God put Peter into the trance, preparing him. When Cornelius' men arrived, Peter was ready.

As Peter met with Cornelius, the meaning of the vision became clear: there was no favouritism with God. His blessings were for *all* people. Another Pentecost experience took place as the Spirit fell upon Cornelius, his household, and all who had heard the message. Salvation is a gift – offered to the whole world. When God gives us a vision, a dream, may we be always open to his leading.

Prayer

In all that takes place today, Lord, help me to be receptive to your voice.

Encourager

While they were worshipping the Lord and fasting, the Holy Spirit said, 'Set apart for me Barnabas and Saul for the work to which I have called them' (v. 2).

Barnabas went to Tarsus, bringing back Saul to Antioch – the centre of Christian activity. As they preached there, the worshippers came to be known as 'Christians' (Acts 11:26). But they felt the need to spread the Word to others. And so, with John Mark as their helper, they were *sent on their way by the Holy Spirit* (13:4).

At each place, Saul's strategy was to enter the synagogue and proclaim the good news of Jesus Christ to the Jews first. Only when the message was rejected does Saul – *who was also called Paul* (v. 9) – turn to the Gentiles. Jewish opposition soon forced Barnabas and Paul to move onward – to Iconium, Lystra, Derbe. Upon returning to Antioch, they sought to resolve the issue of how to integrate newly converted Gentiles into previously all-Jewish congregations.

The Holy Spirit mentions Barnabas before Saul, when calling them on that first missionary journey. Barnabas could have easily tried to be the leader; after all, he'd been the church leader at Antioch, recruiting Saul as his 'assistant'. He could have become envious of Paul's leadership skills. But Barnabas had been given a priceless gift: that of being an *encourager*. In fact, his name means 'son of encouragement'. He recognised Paul's leadership and rejoiced in it. Encouragement is such a needed gift in the Church.

Missiologist Ralph Winter gave his life to alerting Christians to the world's 'hidden people'. He tells us our globe contains over 17,000 areas that still need to hear of Christ. More than two billion people have no access to the gospel. What can we do? We can each be an encourager; praying, supporting those who *are* able to spread the gospel abroad. We can support those evangelising in our inner cities and communities. We can encourage those going through difficult times. Let's be encouragers – always!

Cherish Wisdom

Keep my commands and you will live (v. 2).

It's so important to cherish wisdom. We must guard it, making sure all decisions we make are wise and of God. The first five verses here make a strong appeal for wisdom. The writer says that words we use are to be wise, not frivolous. We're to keep God's *commandments* and his *teachings*; for when we do we will be able to make wise choices. We are to *call understanding your kinsman* (v. 4) so that we'll not make snap decisions; rather, to be wise in all we say and do. What are we then to do with God's words to us? What of his instructions, through his Word?

Write them on the tablet of your heart (v. 3).

For when the heart is filled with godly wisdom we'll be able, with the help of God's Spirit, to resist temptation. Yes, we cherish *godly* wisdom like we do a *sister*, a close relative, an intimate friend.

We're all tempted. Whether it be a sexual temptation, or something to do with money, or even relating to power and authority over others; temptations *will* come. And Satan knows exactly where to attack – where we're vulnerable, weak. For temptation is seductive, always out to pull us down. This is why the writer tells us to *guard* against things that are not of God.

Evil is never still, but is always moving about – lurking in the shadows, wanting to trap then enslave. And this same temptation is usually dark and secretive:

. . . at twilight, as the day was fading, as the dark of night set in (v. 9).

God wants us to be victorious over temptations; to be discerning, to cherish wisdom from above. Let's *always* come before the Lord, in complete humility, seeking his daily wisdom for our life.

The King of Love

The LORD is my shepherd, I shall not be in want (v. 1).

Many hymns have been written to complement Psalm 23, probably the most favoured psalm of all. Our hymn for today, written by Henry Williams Baker almost 150 years ago, begins:

> The King of love my Shepherd is, Whose goodness faileth never;
> I nothing lack if I am his And he is mine forever.

> *(SASB 53)*

The imagery of the shepherd and his sheep is a striking one. The actual reference to *sheep* occurs, in the King James' Bible, 187 times; the reference to *shepherd*, forty-three times. We're those sheep, who often go astray. But the Lord always makes a way for us to return. We hear his voice, identifying it clearly as *our* Shepherd. And somehow, we instinctively know that we'll be cared for and will do well if we return to the fold. Also, there's something about sheep – about us – that wants to nurture others. We follow the example of the Shepherd. Verse 3 says:

> Perverse and foolish oft I strayed, But yet in love he sought me,
> And on his shoulder gently laid And home rejoicing brought me.

'On his shoulder' – beautiful, isn't it? For he calls us, then leads us to where it's safe, secure; and he carries us to where we'll be nourished and fed. He welcomes us, *rejoices* over us. His staff gently guides us – directing, comforting, loving.

As we read this familiar psalm again, and as we sing this beautiful hymn, especially its last verse, may we celebrate together the Lord's goodness, anticipating living in his house – forever!

> And so through all the length of days Thy goodness faileth never;
> Good Shepherd, may I sing thy praise Within thy house forever.

My Redeemer Lives

'All my intimate friends detest me; those I love have turned against me'
(v. 19).

Sometimes bad things happen to good people. We see it all around us. And sometimes certain people seem so alone. It's heartbreaking, for often we don't know what to do to help alleviate the pain and grief. Suffering of any kind is difficult. Millions of people starve to death, every day. Then there are the *natural* catastrophes that cause such suffering – earthquakes, flooding. There's human-made suffering – war, abuse, violence.

Job's suffering was great, to the point of him feeling his friends had turned against him and deserted him. Physical, emotional, spiritual pain and agony . . . it was almost too much to bear, as he cried out *'Why?'* over and over again. His friends continued in trying to impart their personal wisdom. Yet their words were of no help; in fact, they were beginning to bring him down even further.

The most difficult part for Job was God's silence through it all:

'Though I cry, "I've been wronged!" I get no response' (v. 7).

Then, something suddenly comes over him. The suffering doesn't simply vanish. But something warms his heart; something lets him know that God is very much present. A peace – not of this world – comes upon him. An affirmation from One who knows all about suffering. Love from Father, to child; to the point where Job can look up from his grief, his agony, and say:

'I know that my Redeemer lives . . . in my flesh I will see God . . . How my heart yearns within me!' (vv. 25–27).

How long must suffering continue? Will there be an end? God is Sovereign; he knows all things. We can be certain that he loves us, more than we could ever imagine. Will we trust him, completely?

Gold

'Yet I am not silenced by the darkness, by the thick darkness that covers my face' (v. 17).

Job listened, over and over again, to the untrue attacks by his friends. Now, into the third 'cycle' of debates, his reaction turns into bitterness. He sought out God, the only One who could examine his case and pronounce a fair verdict. But he couldn't find him. Job felt God had withdrawn, leaving him completely desolate.

Yet, he still clung on to a small flicker of hope. Job had experienced God in the past, in a profound way. Although all this adversity was beyond his grasp, and the words from his friends were far from being comforting, he knew deep down God was somehow in it all. Through all the severe trials, Job was still able to say:

'When he has tested me, I shall come forth as gold' (v. 10).

Scripture often uses the image of the furnace to describe God's purification. It's important to know that Job's life was pleasing to God, even before he went through the 'furnace'. The purpose always is for purification. As painful as it might be, when it happens to us, we'll be both refined and purified – if we trust God implicitly. We, also, will come forth as gold.

Many people today lose their faith because of suffering. There are no easy answers. Yet God is just as present when things are going wrong, as he is when things are going well. To have faith during difficult times is infinitely more precious; for it comes from the deep recesses of the soul. What the self decides to do, during these crucial times, is ratified in eternity. When we choose God, somehow, there is a deeper experience of salvation.

The furnace. The purifying fire. But then, through faith, the gold. May we ever keep strong in our faith – through the good times, and also through the mystery of the perplexing times.

Integrity

'I'll not deny my integrity even if it costs me my life' (v. 5, MSG).

Life is often difficult. At some point, most of us go through certain tough times. It might be the loss of a job, or getting into debt. It could be a child who does something hurtful, or a spouse who lets us down. Sickness can strike, even the death of someone close. Life *does* get strenuous. And sometimes grief is overwhelming.

The book of Job is given to us as an example of a man who greatly suffered – probably more so than most – while still holding on to his integrity. Yes, he got angry, depressed, distraught. Yet he didn't lose hope. His world tumbled in; but he kept strong:

'I'm holding fast to my integrity and not loosening my grip' (v. 6, MSG).

The Arabs have a proverb: 'All sunshine makes a desert.' No one wishes bad things upon anyone. But life won't always be easy. The important point is, and perhaps this is the essence of the whole book of Job, when things *do* get tough, how will we react? Will we, like Job, hold on to integrity of the heart? Will we still trust God for the future? Will we get through, because of our faith?

When trials come, it's important to look inward – to make sure there are no hidden sins. To make sure we daily ask for cleansing and forgiveness. To be a person of integrity before God.

Job had an extremely difficult time, deeply questioning why God would allow all this to happen to him. He was human, therefore bewildered by it all. He wrestled within. Yet he remained loyal to God. Why? Because he still believed God created and fashioned him.

Spiritual integrity of the heart is being true to God, no matter what happens to us in life. Let's pray that we'll be men and women of integrity – this day, and all the days to follow.

Conflict Resolution

They had such a sharp disagreement that they parted company (v. 39).

They were ready for what later came to be known as Paul's second missionary journey. But there was a problem. Barnabas wanted John Mark to go with them. Yet John had 'deserted' the team before. Paul felt he'd be a hindrance. So Barnabas parted company, taking John Mark to Cyprus. Paul chose Silas to revisit the established churches, then to spearhead the gospel advance into Europe: Philippi, Thessalonica, Berea, Athens, Corinth.

Personal conflict is not a pleasant thing. But we all face it, at some point or another. Many try to escape it, if at all possible. Yet really, to avoid disagreements is to stop talking altogether. It's bound to come. How we deal with it is the key.

We can take several things from this passage. First, there seems to be no bitterness coming from the disagreement. Paul felt *led* to not include John Mark, fearing for the mission. Barnabas felt *led* to give John Mark a second chance – and Paul recognised their contribution to the extension of the kingdom in his later letters. Second, two missionary parties went forth – each with special qualifications for its respective field of service. Third, the way the conflict was resolved had no ill effects on the whole of the Church. And finally, the incident opened up the door for Silas to be developed as a leader in the gospel ministry.

Conflict resolution is necessary, for there *will* be conflicts and disagreements. But with them, there can be Christian grace and charity. Whether it be in a church situation, or even with family or friends, God has given us all unique and special personalities. When conflict arises, we must seek resolution, beneficial to all.

Thought

If there has been recent conflict in your life, talk it out with someone you trust – and seek the Lord's guidance for resolution.

Ministry Style

'For I have not hesitated to proclaim to you the whole will of God. Keep watch over yourselves and all the flock of which the Holy Spirit has made you overseers' (vv. 27, 28).

Paul finishes his second missionary journey, and is ready for the third – his final expedition. This last one would cover four years, three of these in Ephesus itself. It would involve about a dozen travel companions, exploring new and exciting adventures. At the end of the journey, Paul decides to sail past Ephesus, to avoid spending time in Asia. But, from Melitus, he sends for the elders of the church at Ephesus and bids them a tearful farewell. It reveals Paul's heart, his love for the people there.

In today's Scripture passage we gain great insight into Paul's ministry style. Whether we be a Salvation Army officer, a minister, a church leader, or a young person striving to be a good Christian, this *style* of ministry is not just meant for Paul. It's for *all* – demonstrating the characteristics needed to be effective ambassadors for Christ.

It was a ministry of *transparency*. Paul's life was an open book, no hidden agendas. He made himself available to *all*; ready to speak in larger settings, or one on one. His ministry was one of success; but also of *tears*. Yes, to celebrate; but also to weep with others.

Paul's ministry showed that he was *available*. Whether it be Jew or Gentile, night or day, he was ready. Whether it be meeting someone for coffee, or being prompted to give someone a call, availability is crucial. And finally, Paul's ministry was *selfless*. It was all for Jesus, and the extension of his kingdom. Not drawing attention to self, but rather to be ready, giving totally to others.

Sometimes when we think of 'ministry style' we might think of great preaching or skilled leadership. Both are important. But above all, God wants us to be his instruments, ready to be used for him – in whatever way he desires. Serving with humility and joy in our hearts, may our *style* be always pleasing and acceptable to the Lord.

Triumph

My God, my God, why have you forsaken me? (v. 1).

The psalm for today begins with a sense of real desperation and desolation. It's the deep cry from one who knows God, yet is questioning where he is – during such times of isolation and aloneness. The notion of forsakenness isn't easy, for it can both suffocate and consume. David probably wrote this psalm when being pursued by Saul. Jesus echoed these same words when hanging on that cruel cross, bearing the sins of the world.

Many of us suffer. Whether it be physical, emotional or spiritual pain, the feeling of abandonment is the most difficult part; the feeling that sometimes we're deserted by friends, family, even God himself. Yet the psalmist quickly reminds us that God *is* with us, and has been from the beginning. A few verses later we read:

And to think you were midwife at my birth, setting me at my mother's breasts! When I left the womb you cradled me; since the moment of birth you've been my God (vv. 9, 10, MSG).

The Lord is there, and always has been. He understands our human-ness, as we cry out to him. It's part of the journey we're all on, together. Yet, because he wants us to reach out of ourselves, and think also of others, the last part of the psalm gives an outward vision as it gives ultimate praise to God. As Christ turned his own forsakenness into rapturous, eternal joy, we – as his brothers and sisters – must now be on fire to carry forth the gospel message:

From the four corners of the earth people are coming to their senses, are running back to GOD. Long-lost families are falling on their faces before him. GOD has taken charge (vv. 27, 28, MSG).

Are we ready, and willing, to help bring triumph to a world that is in desperate need of Christ? May it be so today!

Softly and Tenderly

We who are still alive and are left will be caught up together with them in the clouds to meet the Lord in the air. And so we will be with the Lord for ever (v. 17).

S ome might think this beautiful hymn old-fashioned, and therefore somewhat irrelevant for today's fast-paced world. But let's not be too quick to throw out the old for the new. Both have their place. If hymns are of God, they'll speak to the heart of a believer. If you know the tune, perhaps you'd like to sing as an act of worship:

> Softly and tenderly Jesus is calling,
> Calling for you and for me!
> Patiently Jesus is waiting and watching,
> Watching for you and for me!
>
> (SASB 264)

There's an urgency here; for the Lord is waiting for our response to his call. He's not demanding, or forcing; he's calling 'tenderly', as a loving Father. The desperation lies in the fact that it's about life, or death. He wants his children to return, to give their *all* to him. Verse 3 ends this way, assuring us of God's forgiveness:

> Though we have sinned, he has mercy and pardon,
> Pardon for you and for me!

The great evangelist Dwight L. Moody, on his death bed, turned to his friend – the author of this song – Will L. Thompson and said, 'I would rather have written "Softly and Tenderly" than anything I have been able to do in my whole life!' The song, this refrain, says it all. God wants us to be with him, forever! We're destined for home!

> Come home, come home! Ye who are weary, come home!
> Earnestly, tenderly, Jesus is calling, Calling, O sinner, come home!

More Advice

Doesn't the ear test words, as the palate tastes food? (v. 3, HCSB).

Eliphaz, Bildad and Zophar had said their piece. Through three cycles of debates, they imparted their wisdom. But they were of no help, for they spoke their own thoughts, their own ideas – from a human point of view. Their arguments had been exhausted, and were comfortless.

In comes a younger contemporary – Elihu. He feels he can solve the mystery of Job's suffering. So he starts expounding upon the assumption that the Sovereign's actions are educational, not necessarily disciplinarian. He proceeds to give a lengthy defence of God's dealings with humans. His conclusion:

Indeed, it is true that God does not act wickedly and the Almighty does not pervert justice (v. 12, HCSB).

Elihu goes further to deal with Job's most persistent complaints. First: Why be good, if you're going to end up suffering anyway? Second: Why doesn't God listen to the cries of a broken heart? Elihu certainly doesn't have all the answers. But it took this young man to remind Job that God's ways are different from human ways. It's similar to what's recorded in Isaiah:

'For My thoughts are not your thoughts, and your ways are not My ways.' This is the LORD's *declaration (55:8, HCSB).*

God asks us to trust him, in order that he may accomplish his purpose for our life – even though it might involve suffering, tragedy, pain. It's okay to have doubts, fears, questions. But then, it's crucial that we have *faith* to believe, in the end, that God is with us. Yes, it's good to get advice from others – even those younger than ourselves. But ultimately, we must believe God *is* Sovereign, is over all and in all. He loves us more than we could ever imagine. What more can we ask?

Out of the Storm

Then the LORD spoke to Job out of the storm (v. 1).

For thirty-seven chapters, Job waits for the Lord to speak. Finally, he does – *out of the storm*. Rather than answering Job's myriad of questions, God ministers to the need of Job's heart. He commences by giving Job a panoramic sweep of nature. God then bombards Job with questions – resulting in Job being humbled by who God is.

Some scholars call these final chapters a *theophany*, an appearance of God; for God establishes who he is. God of eternity, the universe, of all creation; God of Job, God of you and me. When God speaks, it's probably one of his most profound utterances in all of Scripture. For it's a revelation of his identity, his purpose, and ultimately his great love for each one of us.

Swiss psychologist Dr Paul Tournier writes: 'For God's answer is not just an idea, a proposition, like the conclusion of a theorem; it is himself. He revealed himself to Job; Job found personal contact with God.'[8]

We would all like God to speak to us in the sunshine; but sometimes he must speak out of the storms of life. Job said that God had forsaken him – at the time of his deepest need. Yet God was always around him, if Job had only taken the time to look. He became so preoccupied with himself that he lost his perspective – missing God's self-revelation, which exists in all of creation.

No, God did not explain the cause of Job's suffering; but he let Job know that he had been *with* him. Sixteen times throughout the book Job asks *why*. Fifty-nine times we encounter the word *who* in reference to God. Perhaps God felt Job didn't need to know *why*; rather, to know *who* was with him.

May we be fully aware of *who* God is. May we be aware of his profound love for us. May we be aware of his constant desire to be with us, always, and through *all* circumstances of life.

Guarantee

'My ears had heard of you but now my eyes have seen you' (v. 5).

In this last chapter, Job's humbled that God is responding directly to him. He acknowledges God's power and justice in executing his plans, and withdraws his accusations against God. For Job finally realises that whatever God does is right, and we must accept his actions by faith.

The great preacher Charles Spurgeon once said that the door of repentance opens into the hall of joy. Job, even through all his suffering, can still look to his God with a sense of joy in his heart; for he was his servant.

Through perseverance, suffering, faithfulness, integrity – and, yes, even our humanity – we too can become his servants: the people God wants us to be, filled with joy. For only one thing in life is a definite guarantee: not happiness, liberty, wellness, shelter, food, security, not even life itself. The only thing that is an absolute guarantee is the only thing we actually need: God.

Job's knowledge of God before all his trials was primarily second-hand; by the hearing of his *ears* – perhaps from parents, friends. But now, after passing through the fire of adversity, he sees God more clearly, gaining faith and courage to trust him implicitly.

As a reward for his faithfulness, Job receives back from God twice as many sheep, camels, oxen and donkeys. God also blesses him with seven sons and three daughters – exactly the number of children lost earlier. Yet it's not just about receiving material gain. We're to receive spiritual blessings. Job's greatest blessing was his personal encounter with God:

'I know that You can do everything, And that no purpose of Yours can be withheld from You' (v. 2, NKJV).

Prayer

Lord, help me to trust you, always. No matter what I go through, help me to have faith for the outcome. Your love is my guarantee.

Connecting

The following night the Lord stood near Paul and said, 'Take courage! As you have testified about me in Jerusalem, so you must also testify in Rome' (v. 11).

When Paul returned to Jerusalem after his third missionary journey, he knew the possible fate that awaited him. He faced an angry mob, accusing him of false teaching and polluting the temple. Before the crowd he defended himself by sharing his testimony. He then waited to declare the gospel message.

His heart's desire was to share the gospel with anyone who would listen; to communicate with others, telling them of Jesus Christ. He travelled for many years, under very difficult circumstances, telling both Jews and Gentiles of God's love. He was beaten, tortured and imprisoned; but it didn't matter, because it was all for Jesus. Christ's mandate for Paul is also ours. But how can we effectively communicate and connect with others?

Advances in communication have been astounding since the 1800s. The fastest communication available in 1840 was Samuel Morse's electric telegraph. The invention of the telephone followed in 1876; television broadcasts began in 1930; computers were sold commercially in 1951; the fax was introduced in 1966; cellular phones were used in 1979; and the mind-boggling World Wide Web was launched in 1989, making communication and connections happen at the speed of light. New breakthroughs and discoveries are still happening even as I write these words. We're constantly demanding a *faster* world, to connect more efficiently.

Paul did all he could to connect with people, to communicate the message of Christ. It eventually cost him his life; but he could do nothing less. It was part of the fabric of his being. We are also mandated to share the message of Jesus. Connecting with others is vital.

Prayer

Father, help me to connect with people today on a deep, spiritual level. Whether in conversation, or by email or letter, I want to let others know of your everlasting love – that will change their lives forever!

Love Cannot Fail

Then Agrippa said to Paul, 'Do you think that in such a short time you can persuade me to be a Christian?' (v. 28).

Following Paul's dramatic conversion on the road to Damascus, the apostle did all he could to follow God's direction for his life. But it wasn't easy. He faced extreme opposition everywhere he went. Yet in facing constant conflict and persecution, he remained faithful – and people's lives were changed, forever. He was obedient, and God was ever present.

The known world became a different place. Pockets of new Christian believers began to spread the gospel, willing to give their lives for Christ. It was all because they had accepted God's unconditional love for them. And love cannot fail.

Paul expressed his love through times of turmoil. Even through stoning, beatings, imprisonment, he was always there for others – all because of love. People are still being persecuted for their faith today. They need our support through prayer and intercession.

Paul expressed his love through encouraging others. The newly established churches needed encouragement to keep strong and firm in their faith. There's nothing quite like a word of hope and encouragement from another! It's vital, and life-giving.

Paul expressed his love through a humbleness of spirit. He was attacked, accused, abused. Yet love prevailed. Love cannot fail, especially when it's showered upon those who express unkindness and hostility. Humility is not a weakness, but a strength; for it shows a strong sense of the inner self, because of God's Spirit.

Finally, Paul expressed his love through his strong witness. When we're in communion with our Lord, his love is ever present. And so, as we bring closure to this book, it's wonderful to end with the subject of *love*. I now leave you with my blessing:

> **May the Lord continue to bless you and keep you;**
> **May his love radiate in and through you;**
> **May you sense his peace, hope and love, always. Amen.**

Notes

1. Augustine, *Confessions*, trans. Henry Chadwick, Oxford University Press, 1991.
2. Elie Wiesel, *All Rivers Run to the Sea: Memoirs*, Knopf, New York, USA, 1995.
3. Brother Lawrence, *The Practice of the Presence of God*, Doubleday, New York, USA, 1977.
4. William Booth, *Purity of Heart*. First published 1902, revised edition published by Salvation Books, International Headquarters, London. © 2007. The General of The Salvation Army.
5. Dietrich Bonhoeffer, *The Cost of Discipleship*, SCM Press, 1959.
6. Peter Adam, *Speaking God's Words: A Practical Theology of Preaching*, Regent College Publishing, Vancouver, Canada, 2004.
7. John Gowans, *Musical Salvationist*, vol. 99. © Salvationist Publishing and Supplies Ltd, 1985.
8. Paul Tournier, *Guilt and Grace*, Harper & Row, New York, USA, 1962.

Index

Subscribe . . .

Words of Life is published three times a year:
January–April, May–August and September–December

Four easy ways to subscribe
- By post – simply complete and return the subscription form below
- By phone – +44 (0) 1933 445 445
- Online http://sar.my/wolsubu (for UK) or http://sar.my/wolsubo (for overseas)
- Or visit your local Christian bookshop

SUBSCRIPTION FORM

Name (Miss, Mrs, Ms, Mr)..
Address ....
....Postcode ....
Tel. No. ....
Email* ....

Annual Subscription Rates
UK **£12.50**   *Non-UK* £12.50 + £3.50 P&P = **£16.00**
Please send me .... copy/copies of the next three issues of *Words of Life*
commencing with **September–December 2012**

Total: £ .... I enclose payment by cheque ☐
Please make cheques payable to *The Salvation Army*

Please debit my Access/Mastercard/Visa/American Express/Switch card

Card No. ☐☐☐☐ ☐☐☐☐ ☐☐☐☐ ☐☐☐☐ Expiry date: ___/___

Security No. ☐☐☐   Issue number (Switch only) _____

Cardholder's signature: .... Date: ....

Please send this form and any cheques to: **The Mail Order Department, Salvationist Publishing and Supplies, 66–78 Denington Road, Denington Industrial Estate, Wellingborough, Northamptonshire NN8 2QH, UK**

☐ *We would like to keep in touch with you by placing you on our mailing list. If you would prefer not to receive correspondence from us, please tick this box. The Salvation Army does not sell or lease its mailing lists.